NOT BY CHANCE

KORI MOORE

NOT BY CHANCE

A POETIC CELEBRATION OF GOD'S GREATEST GIFTS

Tate Publishing & *Enterprises*

Not By Chance
Copyright © 2008 by Kori Moore. All rights reserved.

This title is also available as a Tate Out Loud product. Visit www.tatepublishing.com for more information.

No part of this publication may be reproduced, stored in a retrieval system or transmitted in any way by any means, electronic, mechanical, photocopy, recording or otherwise without the prior permission of the author except as provided by USA copyright law.

The opinions expressed by the author are not necessarily those of Tate Publishing, LLC.

Published by Tate Publishing & Enterprises, LLC
127 E. Trade Center Terrace | Mustang, Oklahoma 73064 USA
1.888.361.9473 | www.tatepublishing.com

Tate Publishing is committed to excellence in the publishing industry. The company reflects the philosophy established by the founders, based on Psalm 68:11,
"The Lord gave the word and great was the company of those who published it."

Book design copyright © 2008 by Tate Publishing, LLC. All rights reserved.
Cover design by Kandi Evans
Interior design by Jonathan Lindsey

Published in the United States of America

ISBN: 987-1-60696-295-4
1. Poetry: Inspirational, Religious
08.10.21

"When attempting to be more than simply one is, confinement ensues and freedom is lost."

NOT BY CHANCE

You spoke words into my being
and life into my lungs,
From the ashes I came and You being
God gave me a pretty name.
When my spirit was growing weary
and my eyes were growing dim,
You whispered, "Hush, my child, your
journey is soon enough to end."
You filled up my thoughts and gave me the will
to live, then when life seemed too tough You
were always there to lend a helping hand.
Therefore, I dedicate my life to You,
Your service, and Your dance.
I love You, God, Creator of all, my
being here isn't by chance.

THE ATONING SACRIFICE

There is a day of judgment that awaits us all.
It wasn't this way from the start but
has been this way since the fall.
The time we spend here on this earth
is mere vanity, indeed, if you're not pre-
pared and ready to face eternity.
In our lives we've turned away and fol-
lowed after sin, but God has loved us from
the start and wants to bring us back again.
He came to earth a humble man,
the atoning sacrifice,
and although you were dead in your
sins He paid the ultimate price.
On the cross He thought of you as
tears streamed down His face
He said, "My child, here I am
dying to take your place."
Like a lamb does not cry out so
He made not a sound
but took your sins upon Himself
as He wore a thorny crown.
The wrath of God fell on Him
as He became your sin;

every lash that he faced was
caused by your rebellion.
He gave up His spirit when it was time
and committed Himself to the grave, but
death couldn't hold Him; His love was
too strong as He thought of you again.
He rose from the grave and is preparing a
place somewhere in the great beyond,
So don't let sin or the things of this earth
keep you from where you belong.

HOPEFULLY

I believe that all language, though cultivated by man, can be used to heal
the earth in the right hands.
I believe in the sun...God of heat and fire.
I believe in passion and domesticated desire.
I gave myself to study truth the only
way I could and realized my own shortcomings, as only I would.
I noticed nothing new abounds in the
way of words, but if you don't speak what
you feel, how else will you be heard?
And so I chose at an early age to
make my causes known—
I chose to be a poet...my thoughts
and emotions to show.
So here I am writing today with nothing much to say...but hopefully the nothing I speak will lighten another's day.

MOTHER EARTH

She is a work of art.
She models for the moon.
She has an ancient history, but her
end may come too soon.
She gives us all her love, and in her heart is found
the beating of a drum to the distant sound—
Of waves gently falling onto the ocean floor.
The life beat of the world turns round
and round within her core.
I speak of our mother, I speak of the birds,
I speak of the trees...I speak of the earth.
She whispers in our ears and sings
through the breeze, but she is growing old and is plagued with a disease.
Humanity has more, you see,
than just one dire need.
Using up her resources—trading pleasure for mere greed.
So she continues giving, while we continue taking, never realizing even for
once what a mistake we are making.
Endlessly she soars through space
with a galaxy to contend.

She is called by many names, but me, I will call her friend.

JUBILEE

The moon is setting—dawn is drawing near.
On the horizon...purple and
orange—everything is clear.
The fog is breaking, the rain has ceased,
and the shrimp boats are all out to sea.
I'm alive if only for now...to witness this jubilee.

THE MURAL

The neon signs were red and yellow as I made my way down the dimly lit corridor...I found my room.
The flashing lights blinked incessantly on and off as I entered.
The hotel was cheap, and I paid to leave my mark.
White and longing for completeness there it stood...pure and unblemished, so I began to experiment (with colors of course).
First blue then green.
The landscape came alive...painting itself.
Vivaldi swayed to and fro with the movement of my hands...echoing through my mind as I shaped the clouds to my liking.
Then?
It was complete.
I stood there for a moment in silent appreciation of my own endeavors.
I packed my things and was gone as quickly as I had arrived...red and yellow lights still flashing in the distance.

LOVE DIVINE

The flowers all play music...as
I lay beneath the sun.
Every one a different flute, but I have chosen one.
Pink and blue it smiles at me
and beckons me to come.
And so I rise to my feet and
move to where it's from.
Quietly I pick and laugh while
making not a sound.
How much joy it brings to me
with no one else around.
The flower exists to brighten days,
and today it brightened mine.
Oh, how pleased I am now found
because of love divine.

SOMETHING NEW

I don't want to fall asleep...the
day is much too grand.
My life with you is so much more
than I could have ever planned.
You give me meaning...you give me
hope...you give me strength to fly.
I want you to know every waking hour
what you have done for me inside.
You picked me up and dusted me off and made
me feel a jewel.
I thank my God for the gift of life
but mainly for the love of you.
You are the reason I wake up and
the reason I can sleep.
I love you because you under-
stand...you mean the world to me.
Life with you is never dull, there
is always something new.
And so I will spend the rest of my
days...simply loving you.

JESUS

I felt so alone in the world with no one to attend.
No one I could turn to, no one
I could call My friend.
My disciples they all ran away
when My hour came.
They denied ever knowing Me
and even denied My name.
But I was bruised for their transgressions and crushed for their iniquities.
The sins they had committed fell directly upon Me.
I know what it means to hurt, to cry, and to bleed.
So in your hour of sorest need,
I beg you come to Me.
I've walked the walk and talked
the talk all for you to see.
Then the Father in His great mercy
chose to place Me on a tree.
You see, the Lord did not withhold His Son
and this was His great joy...to give Him freely
to the world, so won't you to Him employ?
All He asks is all that you are
and all you have to give.

He can make your life worthwhile and teach you how to live. He'll be walking right by your side wherever you may go. There's nothing standing in your way...don't you think it's time to grow?

JUST ME

He was brilliant and shapely with a smile
that could lighten the darkest day.
When he said my name, it was like the sun;
when he touched my hand, it was like the rain.
He was a connoisseur of love;
he drank it like wine.
He was reckless in wild abandon-
ment and believed in possibilities.
The world was always his friend.
He was veiled with childish laughter and his
soul danced beneath gold-tinted flesh.
I wish I could be more like him
but realize I'm just me.
It's enough to know that kind of love
exists and that sets my spirit free.

NEW BIRTH

New beginnings means new
birth...spirit, water, and fire.
Just pilgrims on this path called life,
climbing ever higher and higher.
When Jesus came, He said, "Follow where I lead."
Instead of passing out riches that day,
He passed out the people's needs.
Peter had it right when he said, "Money have
I none, but as I have I give to you, to each and
every one."
To say that He's more precious than silver,
more costly than a jewel, is an understatement
to say the least after all He can do for you.

TIME

Trapped within language, trapped within mind,
Trapped within nothingness, but
not trapped in rhyme.
I hear you call out...a voice locked within—
The wind chimes are blow-
ing, I'm growing closer to Him.
How can I move if movement's delayed, or how
could I sing if no voice was arrayed?
The God of the Heavens, the God of the earth,
is found within doors and alive in the church.
I quiet myself nothing as I lay down for bed,
but sudden destruction is found in my head.
Angels have plenty while merry men whine, but
these are just thoughts...I'm just killing time.

IN THE DAYS OF YOUR YOUTH

Sometimes in oneness you are aware that the
universe is centered as you breathe in God's air.
Sometimes your heart, when roused by a dream,
plays goofy games that are without a name.
Sometimes in moments of sheer ecstasy
your spirit flies free and rests in the sea.
But when you're alone and are basking in sun,
what do you think of when your heart is undone?
I hope that you think of the love
that you've known and in moments
like these treasure and own—
All of the beauty you witness around from the
green of the fields to the magic of sound.
Remember your Maker in the days of your youth
and you will be blessed in whatever you do.

THE UNKEPT GRAVE

As I make my way down many columns
and rows, many numbers and names, something near the back catches my eye.
There, under a tree, concealed by rampant weeds, stands a small granite rock.
The name is unclear...worn by
years of wind and rain.
You were such a large part of someone's life, yet the headstone appears small
and unimportant among many others.
Shapely the rock, yet nothing to draw much a second glance—the only remnant of your existence.
Just a simple stone in the corner to remind
us of your life here on earth—you exist now
in the form of a label—a tag...lot 151.
You were, I'm sure, loved by many, but as generations passed, memory of you did the same.
So this is all that remains—an unkept
grave—alone but not forsaken, unnoticed but not forgotten.
Don't feel alone, sweet soul...you were remembered today in the heart and mind of a stranger.

THE CEREMONY

The circle has many a face.
The square is much prouder found.
The circle lies in fields of gold,
While the square is nowhere bound.
So to you I give this circle of
love, none other to impart,
For you, being no square at
all...up and stole my heart.

NEGLIGENCE

I watch as a child rides down
the street dodging traffic.
No helmet...no protection.
Where's his mother?
She's inside watching soaps while
her child plays in the road.
Yep, while she's inside watch-
ing "Days of Our Lives"
Her child is outside watch-
ing "The Last Day of His Life."

THE LIFE OF A TREE

Winter has settled...alone I stand—tall
and majestic but alone nonetheless.
Oh, little boy, come back to me...you've
shared with me your secrets, you've
shared with me your tears.
Oh, little boy, come back to me, climb on my
shoulders and I'll hide you once more from the
screaming of parents and an unclean room.
What's college?
I'm afraid I don't understand.
That's okay ...
I hear you're coming home this week-
end to help Dad ready the yard for the new
pool that's to be installed next week.
New pool...ha, I still say the
yard is much too small.
Wait, is that a car door I hear?
Footsteps coming this way?
My dearest child...most precious friend—
Why, you are no longer a child
but have become a man.
It's so good to see you, but why do
you carry that axe in your hand?

WHY?

We're growing up now, and time passes us by
like an hourglass of images painted by the sun.
It seems as if eternity is gone, and we're left
with a leaflet of uncertainty, while wait-
ing for a tomorrow that will never come.
I hold today with thoughts of yes-
terday, but will I ever be young again
when the youth in me has fled?
It's funny how things go in life,
with the fleeting of a glance.
I long for what I had before but
know I can't go back.
Caught by this dream, I recline back
and sigh…I long for all the answers but
know I'll die still wondering why.

THE PATH I'VE TROD

Sweet melody abounds in me
as time resides in God.
I chase away the pain of life
while resting on this log.
I contemplate the sky above and
the ground beneath my feet.
The trees they sway to and fro
as I drift off to sleep.
I will focus on my dreams while
longing for the peace
I've found nowhere else in life
except down on my knees.
When I awake it will be to the
sound of nature at its best,
And so not a care have I in life
from one day to the next.

NO MATTER WHERE YOU ARE

Our love cannot be shaken, it's
stood the test of time.
It's far beyond all reason, and
far beyond all rhyme.
You seem to me a world away,
but always close at hand.
You're like a beautiful sun-
set...you're like a distant land.
You seem to me just out of
reach, like a passing star,
But I will keep on reaching for you
no matter where you are.

ONE DAY

He was a poet with quiet hands…He
was an artist in barren lands.
He played the guitar, he played the drums.
He walked through life but wanted to run.
I gave him my love, I gave him my heart, I gave
him my soul, but he wanted a fresh start.
He lived in the woods, he lived by the sea,
but his spirit was caged far beneath me.
He painted many pictures but couldn't explain
why it seemed like he was in so much pain.
I told him if he would love, I told him if he
would laugh, I told him if he would open
up, he would find life's treasure map.
He poured out his heart, and
tears were in his eyes.
I smiled to myself and thought,
One day, man, you will fly.

HE WILL MAKE YOU SING

The sun is brightly shining…the
grass is growing high.
The fields are alive with melody, and I am alive inside.
My spirit is ablaze, my soul is filled with praise,
My heart is filled with laughter as on my knees I pray.
I know a higher power, you can call him God.
He's been my friend since I was born
and fills my days with song.
So if you don't know happiness or
the joy that life can bring,
Submit yourself to Jesus and
He will make you sing.

MOTHER

She's a mother—she's bored.
She lives with a husband—who snores.
With graduation near—the future's unclear.
What did she do to end up here?
What happened to youth?
What happened to dreams?
There's nothing left for her, it seems.
So here she's left standing, with
a life too demanding—
In a kitchen too small by a too wide of hall.
She has dishes to clean, the phone starts to ring.
Supper's at eight, but her husband is late.
The table's not set—the bills are unmet,
So she smiles and sighs, "I can't kill myself yet."

RUSH HOUR

Today on the subway I ignored the
hustle and bustle and spotted a little
girl in the corner selling daisies.
I bought one for charity's sake
and placed it in my hair.
Now a "Flower Child," I birthed a poem ...
It's amazing what a little bit of earth can
do on the concrete highway of life.

ABRAHAM

Abram was a man of God, known
as the "Father of our faith."
Believing God against impossible odds,
determined to go all the way.
Issac was the promised son that he was
asked to give, never even questioning
God Why He would ask this of him.
He raised his knife, but just before the sac-
rifice was to be made, he heard a voice say,
"Now I know you truly fear My name.
Since you have not withheld from Me, even
this your very own son, I will give you a Brand
new name, Abraham will be the one."
The test was over and he prevailed with tri-
umph in his eyes, he knew that life was bet-
ter Lived with the Creator by his side.
A ram was caught in the thicket, a fore-
shadow of things to come, for soon God
Himself Would give His only begotten Son.
He provided the sacrifice back then, and
later in history He would provide once
again by Dying for you and me.

MOM

She was beautiful the way she always was.
The summer sun on her back, the mountains crying over her shoulders.
I never knew true love until I
found her heart for me.
It was in the snow and leaves.
The grass hinting that fall was near—now
came her season, the season of fires and tea.
I loved her that way, cuddled on the
couch, Denver not far off.
She was my friend, my mentor, my teacher, and my mom.

CURSED SKY

The birds have filled the sky with the chirping of
melancholy chants to an ever forgotten moon.
Clowns no longer play by night and the stars
cry for a daybreak they will never find,
But why, Lord, oh, why ...
why have you cursed the sky?

A DAY IN THE PARK

With all the colors of flight she
ran...faster and faster, chasing the object
of her momentary enlightenment.
Grass beneath her feet, flow-
ers between her toes, she ran.
Then...drawn to a sudden halt...it landed.
She caught her breath.
There just overhead on a branch it rested.
A sharp pang of excitement flooded the
child's body, excitement and fear.
What if she lost this dream?
What if she lost her step and this
poor, timid beauty took to wind?
Ever so gently she moved.
Closer and closer.
Quietly...so quietly.
Even the rapid heartbeat within seemed a
threat but now—within reaching distance,
her breathing increases, faster and faster.
The small creature senses danger in
its surroundings, it spots the child but
oddly enough it remains—captured per-
haps by the beauty of her youth.

Desiring contact one with the other it craves
her touch and sacrifices a life of flight.
Hypnotically the creature falls under
the seduction of her frailty and
appears to welcome her grasp.
Hands closing quickly around the
small body bring with them a sud-
den panic and need for escape.
She rejoices and smiles in delight at her
accomplishment, feeling the uncontrol-
lable rustling between her palms.
She is holding life—for the first time she is
holding life, but wait…in her excitement she
hadn't realized how hard she squeezed.
The beating stopped, the movement died,
and just as quickly she began to cry.
I felt the love of life that day
and felt the pain of loss.
I felt the joy that freedom brings and
the price that possession costs.
I learned that if you love something, you
need to leave it be, for it never is as pre-
cious caught as if you'd left it free.

SKIES OF GOLD

In this moment I do delight
and savor the rising sun.
The morning star is fading
fast...night will soon be done.
On the horizon and in my view
all sorts of lovely hues.
From the simplest of oranges to
the purest form of blue.
I deeply breathe a breath of light
and center myself in love.
The ocean waves repeat the sound
of seagulls up above.
The sand beneath that cools my feet
is somewhat calm and moist.
I hear a humming within my mind
and know it is God's voice.
I'm alive and am in His will this
morning of all times.
I'm surrounded by the earth he made
and am trying to pen a rhyme
To explain all the sights and sounds
I feel within my soul.
I witness the rebirth of dawn
and witness skies of gold.

Have you ever held a time so perfectly
unflawed that your spirit leaps for joy
and your voice is alive with song?
If you have then you can relate to what it is I say.
Hold on to those moments with all
your heart don't ever let them fade.
Then when you're down or feel-
ing sad remember them with a smile
They can be your dearest friend and
make living more worthwhile.

EACH DAY

When I hear the chirping of a sparrow, oh,
so kind...I think about the spring of life
and have pleasant thoughts in mind.
When I hear the echoed call of geese
high in the sky...I sing to my Creator
for the simple gift of life.
I see His nature, hear the birds, and
whisper sweet and true, to a calm and
placid sky...cherishing it's blue.
When I drift away in thought and soft-
ness is my friend—I realize in His pres-
ence only sunshine rounds the bend.
So tell me then what care have I for things out of
my hands?
I know all things will work for
good according to His plans.
So I live each waking hour until the
sun has set, knowing in my heart of
hearts each day will outdo the next.

YOUTH'S SWEET GAME

Dancing down by the little town
where a halo of lights are shown
Reminds me of a time I played so long ago
In open meadows with streams and
stones upon the river's edge.
Mighty fortresses were laid about and
were formed by simple hedge.
Those were the days of freedom
and fun basking in the sun.
My soul as a child called out to
God, the living and only One.
I laughed and sang many a
hymn to the rising dawn.
The sparrows were there, the squir-
rels and deer...they all had joyful songs.
The robins all listened with a carefree ear
and the dandelions glowed so bright.
Those were the days of purity,
innocence, and light.
Those were the days I felt so
alive, before a harder time.
Now I have to face the world with
a responsible state of mind.

That's okay, we all grow up, but
the memories still remain.
And so I sway to and fro, remem-
bering youth's sweet game.

LOVE, LAUGHTER, AND JOY

The soft gray calm of morning...sets an even tone,
For the day ahead as the car lights
dimly glow—on the cool dark pave-
ment reflecting radiant beams.
I realize that this life isn't all
that it's cracked up to be.
The ocean is inviting as I drive up by the shore.
I watch the clouds hang overhead
and wonder what this life is for.
Here I sit all alone...there isn't another soul—
parading down the beach—and suddenly I know.
It is for love, it is for laughter, it is
for spreading joy to the people I can't
see but so thoughtfully employ.

FREEDOM

In the blue of desolate dawn the Wildman
roars and lions nibble at his toes.
The grass flows and he wanders with
the sun on his back and land.
He's back in Africa again, chasing trees or dirt
and violently exposing himself to thorns.
Halfway across the world a cowboy yells
and throws up his hat while lying in
sand, but the stars melted for Wildman
last night and poured into earth.
Freedom had won...so had he.

ASK AND YOU SHALL RECEIVE

You sit at the table all day long, begging for bread, but you ask for it wrong.
These are a few things I think you should know about loaves handed out about an hour ago.
The loaves fed the hungry, the lowly...distraught.
Passed out by disciples with fish they had caught.
They reached in their baskets...a miracle to perform, so if you want true bread...ask the Calmer of the storm.

WHEN I'M GONE

My mind was a guinea pig for all the world to see.
My thoughts were arrayed with a colorful disease.
"I became a fabulous opera," as
Rimbaud once would say.
My dreams were too long and so was the day.
Locked out of Eden but blissfully in view,
I walked into my room, followed by you.
If grieving is never long and the band plays on,
then here's a song...play it when I'm gone.

LADY EARTH

They are tearing down the trees God
planted and there is a sore in the earth.
I hear her crying but go off to the village to
write about other important things and people.
I find that few give themselves over to soli-
tude for her advantage but promise they
will live with her again someday.
Someday when the sun decides to show
her his face and the mutants of war have
tired of killing themselves in her space.

ESCAPADES

I want to escape to a place of daisies, where people dance around the sun and the moon. People are naked beneath the dance of devilish light.
I want you to want me but not like
the sea that gives way to life.
Patience is a virtue not a spot for higher living.

HIDDEN AGENDA

The smell of old coats and a dim
lamp permeate my dreams—
"Our Little Secret."
Footsteps in the hall and darkness prevails,
soon to be replaced by light again at silence.
Innocence of ten and a mind twisted
by forty-three years of life.
Praised and adored for the torment of my
youth the capturing of my childhood.
Rage, loneliness, betrayal, and desperation
flooded the halls, drenching everything in sight.
I watched as flames engulfed "Our Closet."
Memories now ashes.
Wind, rain, sun, and new growth springs
forth in the form of city park.
Play, little ones…trample underfoot my childhood.
Frolic, little ones…where you now
stand I was betrayed by a friend.
Laugh, little ones…take no notice
of what this ground has seen.

A TIME TO CHERISH

The fresh morning air echoes through time,
Entering my body and soothing my mind.
It whispers and taunts my body with ease.
A gift from my Maker to cherish and please.

YOUTH

What happened to the days?
What happened to the youth?
What happened to the innocence?
What happened to the truth?
Zigzag go the toes over grassy fields, through
refreshing water, onto distant hills.
Little feet dancing, little feet prancing.
To the sun the child is romancing.
She calls to the breeze, "Hide me, please, from
the pursuit of boys and tarnished knees."
She is free in the hills and free in the land,
but suppertime calls and ruins her plans.
So she will play another day, for the song
within her is strong, and when she is grown
she will know she's been playing all along.

THE FUTURE

Gladness, maybe sadness...I suppose it not much to matter
Traipsing down hallways of unwanted wear
I tiptoe...careful not to wake the babe.
Dreamer's doors...what is destiny here?
Thought's choice.
Stone cavities arrayed in the unconscious aura.
Freedoms release...nightly ritual claims perspective life.
Rest...morning calls—soon.
Awake unto dawn, my child, the night
no longer has a hold on you.
Release certain absurdities that
constrict your mind.
Witness the requiem of you life in Polaroid form.
Sail down the streams of experience on the winds of placidity.
Wallow not in yesterday's tragedies, but
serenade the coming of morrow.
Waste not.
Want not.
Throw off the restraints of darkness and
embrace the light...the future is yours today.

FOR YOU AND FOR ME

The earth is given as a gift to heal our
bodies and set our souls adrift.
Upon the sea of love and life...we escape
all chaos and the chains of night.
Evergreens beckon with no one else around...and
so in silence we're heavenly bound
To worship God, sun, and sea and in
these moments to really believe
That there is life after death with no
more heartache and no more regret.
A place of light where the flowers all
bloom...a place created for me and for you.

PAINTINGS IN SAND

The cosmic layout of the land...fills up
my mind like paintings in sand.
The grass beneath is soft and sound...with
no one abiding and no one around.
The breeze is blowing through the leaves...across
the fields and through the trees.
I walk with flowers upon my feet...a
pleasing day created for me.

HALFWAY HOUSE INCARNATE

The vampires are in the rocking
chairs and the fire's on the stove.
Here I sit, cuddling the halfway house incarnate of a dream I never meant to dream.

US

I'm sending out a message, mak-
ing wishes on the stars,
All in an attempt that you will see
them from where you are.
I know we had something, time won't let it die.
I gave myself to you that night
beneath the star-filled sky.
You penetrated my being like no
other man could reach.
I'm thankful for that moment in
time that bound us for eternity.

FERTILE SOIL

I spoke quite tenderly, but was
plagued with discontent.
I wasn't ungrateful though,
that's not what I meant.
Who came before me and what is new birth.
I thought I'd find the answers
by walking into church.
I wondered, Where sat the true giver of life?
Far, I thought, above all the heartache and strife.
I wondered quite often about the world of old.
A world where I'd heard milk
and honey freely flowed.
I wondered if one as lowly as me could
ever reach Heaven and reach eternity.
Then I came kneeling before Your holy throne.
Begging for mercy because of what
Your servant had sewn.

ALTERNATIVE MINDSET

Inferior words of wisdom and a crimson tide.
Waters rage—pushing in anger
against their captor—the shore.
Dancing reflections on myr-
iad streams... . moonlight.
Whimsical tide lines and banks of plenty.
The secret light, within reach—
yet I refrain...scorching heat means
blistering of the heart.
Madness?
A retreat from reality.
Wading through shallow pools of curiosity.
Shall I bathe in external pleasure?
Or save that for another day?
Apprehension...yes, another day.

AS I

To taste you is a joyous song...played
out in harmony.
To smell you is as sweet of rest
as can be found in me.
To see you brings me colors bright and
to hear you is something grand.
Oh, but to feel you beats all of that
as I take you by the hand.

TRAVELING THROUGH THE DAY

She has the scent of angels, with star-
dust in her hair, but she is missing some-
thing—this maiden, oh so fair.
Is it love, or is it lust, or is it something more?
Is it life, or is it death, beating on her door?
Is it speech, or is it thought that
she has been denied?
Or perhaps maybe the prince to be
who is standing by her side?
Whatever it is I wish her well
as I journey on my way.
Just a humble pilgrim am I...trav-
eling through the day.

GOOD THOUGHTS

Labor of love spinning around.
Your web you've sewn to please.
Isn't it marvelous and oh so grand
to spend the day in ease?
Fresh morning sprinkles on your
face...an ever-so-precious dew.
Here is a poem straight from the
heart...sending good thoughts to you.

HOURS

Nectar, it seems, is sweetest to
bees...as honey to a bear.
I gaily spot a butterfly...gliding through the air.
Nature, it seems, speaks to the earth,
while the birds are free to fly.
Yes, I truly live for now, while hours pass me by.

UNDYING PLANS

I bask in the sureness of one first kiss too late.
I run around this planet and
am known to hesitate.
I feel my knees might buckle, I feel my
tongue is tied, I feel as if my moment's
passed and I have been denied.
Beauteous pleasure, toilsome task...oh, to
praise the sun—and when, in fact, I should
have walked, I found I leapt and ran.
Oh, to worry, oh, to fret for a life out of my hands.
I leave my soul...my spirit aches
and cries "Undying Plans."

APPETITE

Man's hunt.
Beast's hunger.
Carnivores all around.
Man's hunt.
Beast's hunger.
Lions on the prowl.
Man's hunt.
Beast's hunger.
Until you learn to tame.
Man's hunt.
Beast's hunger.
Appetite is the same.

INSIDE

She tiptoes through the tulips
she dances with the rain.
She counts the stars at midnight
and collapses just the same.
She waltzes with the marigolds and
whispers through the pines.
She is the lover of my soul and
the lover of my mind.
She is a child she is a muse she is a friend of mine.
She is the master of serene she is quite divine.
I kiss her in the morning before the twilight falls
And then again at dusk when the evening calls.
The girl within is always there
she's always fun and free.
She wraps me in the sweet-
est love and gently sings to me.
I will know the joy of romance
as long as she's alive.
And so to know one's inner self
brings music to one's life.

BRIGHT DAY

I'm thinking about the garden and
how it ended all too soon.
I'm wondering where my God
is on this afternoon,
I remember the days of innocence—when
all good things seemed to flow—
now sheepskin covers our bod-
ies where nudity once was shown.
Death now courses through our
veins...torment on all sides.
Driven out of house and home,
in deserts we now abide.
We are waiting for a redemp-
tion...God promised us a Son.
And so we can only do our best,
until that bright day comes.

HE'S THERE

When your days are dark and dreary
and the sunshine can't be found,
Realize there's a light within and
glory in the world around.
When sadness overtakes and joy seems so far,
Realize your Creator is right there where you are.
He will offer love, He will offer hope,
He will offer happiness and set your soul
afloat—Upon a sea of placid dreams He'll
bring you to your knees and gently woo
your broken heart until your spirit sings.

A FRIEND

Laughter beckons and comes with
warmth to fill the soul inside.
Happiness with vague remorse is
not just a state of mind.
Peace and love that fill our hearts
are spiritually arrayed
With a joy the spirit gives in rea-
soning for each day.
The fruit of God is always light
there is no darkness found.
Within his presence you will see
how each of these abound.
And so to trust him brings new
growth into a decayed heart.
He can help you win the race wher-
ever you may start.
So don't you think you're bet-
ter off to put your trust in Him,
For just when darkness seems too
much He'll let the light shine in.

KEEP US

Graceful lamb, child of light,
Redeem the weary...bound by the night.
Give us Your blessing, for in it we live ...
Fill us with warmth as we bow once again.
We kneel at Your altar and look for Your face
To shine down from Heavens and offer us grace.
Teach us to love, to pray, and believe
Then teach our hard hearts
how to humbly receive.
You are the master, the potter of clay, keep
us, dear Lord, on the wheel every day.

MY GOD

With all power and great might
He named the starry host.
One by one he beckoned them to
shine on moonlit coasts.
He molded the mountains and formed
the lands according to His plans.
He gives me strength for each new
day and courage just to stand.
He circles the sun each new morn-
ing around the noble globe.
Majesty is born in Him with
all the love He shows.
He rules the earth with iron fists
the planets all resound.
To the sound of such a voice
the angels dance around.
Heaven falls at his feet His kingdom has no end,
He is my God Creator of all but a humble friend.
And so I give my praise to Him
for all that He is due.
For without Him in my life my
sky would not be blue.

ELIJAH AND ENOCH

Elijah was taken up to God,
Elisha was left behind.
He had some work that he must
do until it was his time.
His master left in a glorious way,
with chariots all ablaze.
How marvelous his departure appeared
as glory marked his days.
Enoch was yet another soul who
walked in peace with God.
He was also taken up to Heaven as he trod.
They never knew death, as we never
will who put our faith in Christ
For He came to earth to save the world
so our spirits would never die.

FREELY GIVEN

On a mountain hilltop...overlooking plains,
I call out to the Father and rest upon His name.
He gives me peace, He gives me hope,
He gives me strength to fly.
He wraps me lovingly in his arms
as time goes floating by.
All I need is in His hand...as my soul it kneels.
With a smile He beckons me
until my spirit yields,
I witness love so out of line with
what it is I've known,
But that's the beauty of our God,
we never pay what's owed.

ON THE DAY

Knees scraped and burdened fall-
ing on the ground,
Calling to his Maker for a joy he has not found.
So real in this life is all the hurt
that he has come to know,
But there is a love far beyond this
world that he will soon be shown.
On the day when hope does cling to
his weary soul, he will find peace at
last while traveling streets of gold.

ANOTHER WAY

I venture down wooden paths,
where green reflects the sun.
Not a mockingbird is chirp-
ing...I feel their day is done.
Oh, wretched traveler—forbidding
tongues, marching off to war.
Win the battle, win the siege,
till victory is no more.
Forget thy birth—renew the dawn
and I shall hence to say,
"Until the path leads home again,
I shall pass another way."

LIVING

I've found imagination, yes, my dearest friend, in
the form of laughter...love rounding the bend.
Oh, to crawl upon my knees and
taste the sweetest grass.
I commune with nature's call-
ing, nonexistent to the past.
The daffodils are free to dance,
what a shapely sight.
I taste the earth's sweet mel-
ody...the chorus lasts till night.
I hear the echo in the fields and
dream the day away.
Beneath a blue and enchant-
ing sky, I find a place to play.
The birds chime in while beauty is
much...I find great joy in this.
Oh, for a day so grand in life,
when nothing is amiss.
My stomach churns, my mind is a
mess, but all for fun and games.
And so I sit and worship God...sim-
ply living for today.

GOLD

The stream nearby brings some peace
while the violets are in bloom.
I watch as horses parade the fields
and send loving thoughts to you.
The breeze is soft, the sun is bright, and
I, just for today, am left without a thought
in mind as the butterflies all play.
They dance around these happy hours
with not a sound to make.
So seemingly unworried and
so seemingly unafraid.
I've captured a moment so true to
life that I always want to hold.
A moment in time when spring's
afloat and everything is gold.

SOLOMON

Solomon, as you know, was the wisest in the land.
He sought out to find wisdom
with all the brains he had.
He sought out to find pleasure, he sought
out to have fun, but realized in the end
there's nothing new under the sun.
He saw the toilsome labor of the men in the land.
He even saw the sluggards, who
wouldn't lift a hand.
He said, "Their end's the same,
so what does it matter?"
He discovered it is better to mourn
than to hold much laughter.
Everything has a place, as I'm sure that
you have heard, so in the end he realized the only joy in life is to serve.
Fear the Lord and keep His commandments is what it comes down to.
So now the choice is yours to tell
me, What are you going to do?

A DAY WITH GOD

In a grassy meadow…down upon my knees—
I wrestle with the Father for eyes enough to see.
The days they come and go…in this life I know—
Rainbows are afloat as Mother Nature sews.
Just to be is all I need…living for the now,
Reclining on the pillow green
while sparrows hop around.

THE HONEYMOON

The scent of new love is always the best.
Choking out petals are thorns in the flesh.
The rose is of color and that being red.
The sanctity of sweat lies inside the bed.
These lovers know joy and are truly blessed ...
Bound by an oath to forsake all the rest.

IN THE END

Everybody is different—don't
try to make them you.
They all have a different mind
and a unique point of view.
So love them where they are, don't
ever judge or condemn.
You will find you're a better per-
son for it in the end.

HERE WITH ME

Your scent still lingers on my
brow, I take it all in stride.
You are my hopes and dreams in
life, you captivate my mind.
You touched me with a sweet caress and whis-
pered sweet and true...things that only you
would know, whispered from me to you.
If I ever doubt your love, I will remember
with a sigh...the nights we spent beneath
the stars—the nights I learned to fly.
I am reminded of a promise made not so long ago.
That you would think of me while we
are apart and never let me go.
The time we spent, although it seemed short,
will live on eternally, and so I will live each
waking hour as if you are here with me.

THE ANSWER

What was He thinking as he spoke to the wind?
The voice within beckoned and called unto Him.
"Peace…be ye still …" The fishermen all stared
The winds couldn't disobey Him,
no, they didn't dare.
Who was this Man that even the weather obeyed?
He was born in a manger amongst
straw and some hay.
A gift was given and the greatest gift of all
Was the Savior God sent after we took the fall.
He was a servant when He
should have been served,
He was God's Son but a humble carpenter.
He was a leader, but more than just that,
He has been where you've been
and sat where you sat.
Tempted in all ways just the same as you and me,
The only difference is He lived his life clean.
Free from all sin, He's at the right hand of God.
He's the answer to life's bur-
dens, so won't you come along?
Sing songs of jubilation, sing songs
of liberty, sing songs about our risen
Lord, sing songs of being free.

He knows your every heartache, He knows your every strife, He's the answer to the past and the answer for your life.
So don't wait any longer, give your life to Him today.
He sticks closer than a brother and will never turn away.

POINTLESS WORDS OF WISDOM

Miniature jets of flying glass and fear is sparked.
The search for injuries ends with lack of pain.
Tiny fragments (once a bowl) now appear
as diamonds reflecting sunrays.
The brief scare is over—the star-
tling effect has fled.
I ponder the present situation.
Shattered glass must be picked
up yet not touched.
How to go about such a task?
Only one answer comes to mind ...
Carefully.

THE BEACH

I saw an old retired couple, out
amongst the young.
Their purple shorts and colored hair,
mocked the sorest thumb.
They waded through the shallow waters,
peacefully at that, but missed the beauty in
between because both were blind as bats.

THE GIFT OF LIFE

I was warm and toasty, secure
in my mother's womb.
The angels were talking and speaking in tongues
about what would happen this afternoon.
I felt my tummy tickle within an emo-
tion that was quite new.
Down I went into cold hands sur-
rounded by strangers in a room.
I didn't know what I should do,
should I scream, laugh, or sigh?
Unsure of all that was going on,
I decided I would just cry.
I wanted to go back to that place of
love, the only place I'd known,
Then suddenly I heard a voice that
was familiar, I wasn't alone.
Who is speaking? I thought to
myself. I must see her face.
I quieted down and looked around,
then suddenly I was embraced.
There she was smiling at me, and
I knew I'd be all right.
This was the voice I'd come to love
and now she was in my sight.

She gave me birth, and I can't
explain the love I feel inside.
Just to be near her was worth coming
out to this God-given gift called life.

WONDERLAND

I wind myself around a stream
that twists into a fall.
Bobolinks and butterflies hear my echoed call—
To a heart made of love I know beyond the sun.
Sweet embrace…forget me not as
my spirit comes undone.
Time stands still as I ponder this,
my very own wonderland.
Escaping from reality, I rest within your hand.
Castles in the sky above made
from billowy white …
Wash away the soil of years as I fade into light.

THE ONLY THING

A broken man comes to grips
with what it is he's lost.
He never dreamt the price he'd pay
would be of so great a cost.
His life was changed and rear-
ranged in a simple day.
And so the only thing he's got is prayer to pray.

WEALTH

Sometimes disaster comes with sur-
prise...sometimes money's spent.
Sometimes a heart that lives in
remorse is able to repent.
But there are days when laugh-
ter fades and money can't be found.
In the heart of one that gives
there's light all around.
So cleanse your heart and keep it pure from
all that money buys, for in the realm of
all that's true, wealth is found inside.

DAVID AND GOLIATH

When David saw Goliath, he
saw he was quite big.
But he believed in God and
knew that he would win.
Goliath may have laughed, for
David was so young.
Goliath was a giant and well-
known for being strong.
As you know, David won, he gained the victory.
He earned respect from his foes
and from his own army.
And so no matter what the fear
or how big the giant is,
Just remember, you're in God's hands
and He protects what's His.

BEAUTIFUL CREATION

I could spend an eternity...your features try to trace.
Full of inspiration, I would marvel at your grace.
When time has ceased to be, and
the Heavens are no more—
There exists still beauty sweet and
she lingers round your door.

SUNSHINE

The sun is as timeless as the age of his grace—
The gift of our Father to light up this place.
Without it no warmth...the earth all
alone—would hang its sweet head
for the sorrow she'd know.
It brings inspiration to many a souls, so take
time to cherish the simplicity of gold.
Bask in its brilliance and revel in glee, for this
gift of the Heavens gives life unto thee.

IT'S TIME

She cries uncertain tears as she
thinks of all the years—
Gone by in a flash...she thinks about the past.
The laughter and joy...the pain and regret.
The good times and bad that she cannot forget.
She has a constant longing to cap-
ture what is real and to release all the
heartache that she deeply feels.
What can I do or what can I say to make
you enjoy the warmth of this day?
I cannot offer love, I cannot offer hate, all
I can offer is advice you won't take.
So keep reaching out for a hand you can't grab
and keep shedding tears for a heart that is sad.
I'm here if you need me, I'm not far away.
I'm not here to judge you, you'll
learn that someday.
I'll be a true friend...one who listens and shares.
I want you to know that somebody cares.
You matter to God, you matter to me, you
matter in life, and someday you'll see—
That although you've been down, it's time to arise.
Here come your wings, it's time that you fly.

IF ONLY YOU WILL BELIEVE

I considered myself the lucky one—
never wanting to own a face.
No, faces were for folly, and dis-
honor, and disgrace.
So I wore a mask and paraded around town.
No one even noticed that my
spirit was beaten down.
I found a place to hide away, and
I found a place to cry.
I always wore a smile but was suffering inside.
I cornered myself within a shell—never
wanting to let it show, and so I died pain-
fully with each criticizing blow.
But then I found a strength within to soar
above the pain—I promised myself right then
and there that I would never hurt again.
My body, heart, mind, and soul grew
numb to the world around.
All the tears from all the years
came quickly crashing down.
I learned to walk, I learned to run,
I learned to jump and leap.
Isn't it funny what God can do
if only you will believe?

THE BRIDE

Every day she worships God and
bows to give Him praise.
In this land of meadows vast she
whispers His sweet name.
The flowers all grow in the greenest of fields,
The birds all sing with glee,
Amongst all the beauty she has known
she laughs because she's free.
In her mind and spirit sweet she
rests with the world renown.
Majestically she devours love and
wears a glimmering crown.
She is a queen, but more than that
she is married to her God.
In their world of joy and peace
there is no rain or fog.
She gives Him love and He
returns all that she is due.
Her spirit is bright, her mind is alive,
and her eyes the purest blue.
He longs for the day she will enter his
gate and then he will get to hold
His bride so blameless, faithful, and
true. He will cherish her like gold.

He washes away the sins of her youth
beneath the blood-stained cross.
She is His mouth and hands on earth
and she will never be lost.

ONE EVENING

It was nearly sunset...they held each other tight.
They looked at the stars, they looked at the
moon, they looked in each other's eyes.
The waves were gently crashing on the
ocean floor, I knew this couple, no matter
the cost, would be together forever more.
I watched them from a dis-
tance with tears in my eyes.
I prayed to God to know that love
at least once before I die.
And so I witnessed two bright
stars gliding through the air.
I'm thankful I caught a glimpse of Heaven
with the angels standing there.

NEVER OLD

I could write simple lyrics all day long, but
what good is rhyme without a song?
What good is joy without the sad-
ness you feel, and make believe with-
out remembering what's real?
What good is learning if not to bestow, and
what good is logic except that you know?
What good is light without the dark, and
what good is love without a heart?
What good is sunshine without the rain,
and the happiness outside of pain?
For every action there's an effect and
for every decision...possible regret.
But live every day as if it were your last by
looking ahead and forgetting the past.
Then you will find strength for your soul and
although you grow up...you'll never grow old.

LITTLE JERUSALEM

Little Jerusalem is soft as a rose.
She speaks to the earth in a
way no one else knows.
She dances with rainbows and talks to the sun.
She lies on white satin awaiting her love.
He has gone to a distant land but has
promised her his wedding band.
She wears a ring inside her nose and
waits with bells on her toes.
She is so patient, so kind, and so good,
But by the world she is misunderstood.
She has fought many bat-
tles but she will overcome
And in the end will receive the One.

AND SO I DANCE

Glorious is this day at hand. Life is
pleasant and awfully grand.
I taste the flowers on my tongue and
live for beauty when all is done.
I breathe in deep, a joyous task, and
find contentment as I relax.
Upon a pillow I have made, nestled in pine straw I escape
From a world with too much woe,
and so I watch the lilies grow.
The stream it plays and is nearby while
the little birds fly in the sky.
Nothing is wrong here, there is no hate,
in this world that I have made.
And so I dance with my two feet
upon a warm and earthy street.

ONLY A DREAM

I had a dream when I was young...per-
haps a vision of warmth and sun.
I followed it west...from the east it was born.
It took me to the coast and by bountiful shores.
It took me over mountainous hills and plains.
It took me far north then south again.
Suddenly I awoke with a chill of cold sweat, but
the vision was burning and I could not forget—
That although it seemed real and
warmed me indeed, it was noth-
ing more than a fulfilling dream.

JUST BECAUSE YOU LIVE

What is the point of life if not to lend a hand—to
the lowly and distraught by being just a friend?
Use your talents and use your gifts, for that is
His great plan...to joyously share them with
the earth, and by earth, I mean with man.
There is only one God above
and there is only one you.
Nobody else can share certain
truths, that's for you to do.
So don't hold back and hold inside
what you have to give.
The world will be a better place
just because you live.

I KNOW

I know you still think of me, I
feel you in my brain.
You have come to the conclusion
that all women are the same—
But there was something different in me, a spirit that was true,
A heart that was unblemished,
and a body that was new.
We went our separate ways for one reason or the next, but when you think about me, I think you will agree, I was the best.

DAY BEFORE NIGHT

In silent meditation I begin to pray, thanking my God for the glory of today.
The fields are so green, the sky is so blue, the world is alive, and in my view
Are all sorts of violets, daisies, and blooms caressing the meadows I lie with you.
Upon the earth an ever sweet sound...the beauty of the Father is all around.
And so in these hours we do delight, savoring the gift of the day before night.

UP ABOVE

Sweet aroma (the prayers of saints)
into the Master's nose.
The fragrance tells of sacrifice, per-
secution, and of woes.
They die daily, carrying their crosses
for what they do believe,
Hoping to attain the prize for
those who will receive.
A golden crown awaits them there
in a city made of love,
So store up treasures for your-
self that matter up above.

RENEWAL

Tender heart, whisper truth into the pain I know.
Sweet embrace, speak to me of
a love I cannot show.
Calm me down with gentle words
that age cannot define.
Bring repentance, real and just,
into my state of mind.
Hold me now with colors bright,
for my spirit is growing dim
I need your strength for com-
ing days, so renew me once again.

SAMSON AND DELILAH

When Samson met Delilah, he was taken aback.
Spellbound by her beauty, she
seduced him, that's a fact.
His strength was in his hair, but
soon Delilah found that with it sim-
ply cut Samson would be bound.
They burned his eyes, which had caused
his flesh to be weakened by a girl.
Forced into slavery, this man of God
could no longer see the world.
God teaches us all in differ-
ent ways, for lust is of this earth.
So stop and think before you act
and before you give lust birth.

HIS GREAT PLAN

Whispering the echoes of love into
a boisterous soul is the mighty hand
that formed the streets of gold.
Brilliantly displayed is a fount of light, for all
the redeemed released from darkest night.
Meadows dance and I reside within
a glorious land counting all that lay
behind as loss for His great plan.

WORSHIP AND PRAISE

The madness that I've known ...
The freedom that I've sensed.
The joy within reason that has
made me more blessed.
The forgiveness that I've held ...
The Pain that I've dispelled ...
Makes it quite easy to share truths that I've felt.
Love within boundaries ...
Remorseful regrets ...
Heart-wrenching toils filled with repent,
Backbreaking heartache and the sorrow of days,
All for a lesson in worship and praise.

FREE

Pale evening.
Confusing night.
Captive laughter.
Radiant sight.
In the wooded path abroad
The echo of children rings out in song.
Weary pilgrim, your path is long,
But your Maker is there and
you're where you belong.
In the scheme of an awkward life
Hold your head up while embracing the light.
Morning comes and that with glee,
The storm has passed, now your spirit is free.

THE BATTLE

'Twas a day unlike any other.
Brightly burning was the weather.
Hot and wet was the sun-drenched ground
On which the bodies did lie down.
Summer marked a seasonal change
In our lives that were rearranged.
The birth of panic was in our hands
As we cried for a blood-soaked land.
The sirens they roared and did ring out ...
The sound of the battle was all about.
The end arose and that with great start ...
The death of the world was plaguing our hearts.
Nowhere to run...nowhere to hide—
would it continue or would it subside?
Without His great mercy no flesh
would be saved—oh, the sheer tor-
ment of that summer's day.

I AM

Nature is alive with song as it
echoes through my ears.
I've resolved myself to laugh-
ter as morning soon draws near.
The evening is past, the night has
fled, and I ponder where I stand.
I have now found peace of mind
while praising the great I Am.

STARVATION

I offered myself to immorality.
Hesitantly...it refused.
I chased desire once more.
Again it did not—could not respond.
STARVATION!
Craving grew...appetite soared.
The tormentor offered no friendly hand, so ...
I ripped its arm off, and now?
Now I am satisfied.

MONKEYS ON PARADE

How does it feel?
Repression?!
Young minds.
Constraining masks.
Observance?
Could be.... or an inward calling
S-L-O-W-L-Y
And sadly embraced.
Farewell, youthful ecstasy!
Farewell, blissful purity!
May we never meet again.
The time has come to clone—
The many cloning clowns.
Time to join the big charade:
Of Monkey's On Parade.

AT BAY

Sometimes it falls easy like
rain on a summer's day.
Other times, it's like pulling teeth.
It's right there in front of you, grab
it while you can...it won't last.
It can be your night or it can be your day—
This ever-present storm of
mind...keeping you at bay.

HIS QUEEN

The castle smells extra musty and damp tonight,
perhaps that was the hardest thing to get used to.
I tiptoe down the hall cautiously.
Observing every stone, every crack, every crevice.
He's in the next room playing some-
thing like Bach but in his own right.
The sound echoes through the castle cor-
ridor and into the foyer where I have
found a place to sit on white satin.
I recline and absorb the sound; each note flood-
ing my senses, drowning out the worry of the day.
How did I arrive here?
Just a peasant girl of barely seventeen
with nothing to offer except a friendly
smile and a good sense of humor.
Who would have thought that me, simply a
child, would become ruler of such a great land?
I think of all the broken hearts, I think per-
haps even more of all the women he has
known and wonder what he chose me for.
What could he have seen in me?
A spirit that was true?
A heart perhaps a little scared,
never knowing what to do.

I don't deserve this life I live, but he,
a mighty king, must have seen a jewel
inside, for now I am his queen.

MAMA

Tiny hands and fingers...bloody as still night.
All of her labor...still falling out of sight.
Tiny hands and fingers working to the bone—
Her hard-earned money spent
on tinier hands at home.

SUMMER'S NIGHT

The moon is rising high, the echo is in the fields.
The pastures are ablaze with
love, capturing how I feel.
The wheat is all aglow and twinkles in the light.
Oh, how I feel alive on this summer's night.

WINDS OF FREEDOM

Fly on, dear eagle, fly on—lap the mountaintops that boast of high stature.
Soar upon the winds of freedom.
Nest only for a season and take flight again
to mock a world confined by gravity.
Look on, elk, and envy—curse the hooves
that pattern your life for the field.
You have stretched your neck high,
giraffe, but in vain—you are unable
to reach the desired destination.
Mourn, oh creatures of the deep, whose brief
leaping does nothing more than spurn desire.
The little rabbit takes flight but for a moment,
while the trees of the earth spend a lifetime
in upward growth, but as for you, dear eagle,
soar upon the winds of freedom—majestic
and proud with uninhibited delight.

FANTASY

Beauty found its place in her
amidst the pain and strife.
She has warm hands and a gentle
heart but has sacrificed her life.
"Why can't I know what it means to love or to be
loved more than that?"
She poured her heart as she poured
some tea, then she quietly sat.
She has regrets and has shed some
tears and she feels so alone.
But when her mind wanders to love,
she feels as if she's home.
So she sits and so she dreams and
"escapes" nearly every day.
She never shares who she's "with"
or with whom it is she plays.
Imagination is her dearest friend with fantasy
close behind.
I just see her for who she is...an
angel waiting to fly.

WORTHWHILE

I created the world with My two hands
and made the nations stand.
I formed you in your mother's womb
and included you in My plans.
I thought of you when you were born
and chose you even before.
The light that twinkled in your eyes
was a reflection of Heaven's door.
As a child you lay in bed and I right by your side.
Determined to make you special, I
placed a piece of me inside.
I know your every burden and
I know your every grief.
I am with you in the morning and I
am with you while you sleep.
I know you now as I knew you then
and can say with a smile that although
you've turned away more than once,
"Loving you has been worthwhile."

ALTERED REALITY

She's been delving inside herself for so
long she can't find her way back out.
She searches for meaning, she searches
for hope, she searches for some-
thing while traveling this road.
She's been a prisoner of wrong,
she's been a prisoner of right.
She's been forcing the flow as
she barricades the night.
Trapped within lies…trapped within
truth…trapped within memo-
ries—she finally sees the root.
Was it my past, or was it me
That caused this state of mind
and this "Altered Reality"?
Maybe I'll never know, but maybe I will.
All I know now is it haunts me even still.

A TIME TO HEAL

I surrounded myself with mis-
chief but remained in my room.
It's good to live dormant some-
times inside a small cocoon.
And so I laughed and so I played
all the long days through.
For when you are without all hope,
what else are you to do?
I gave myself to folly...I gave myself to dream.
I chased reality from my mind as
sad as it may have seemed.
I devoted myself to visions...I devoted myself
to prayer...I devoted myself to the make-
believe all while resting in my chair.
We only know the life we live and
we make it all our own.
I'm thankful for that time in life
that really helped me grow.
So don't feel bad to just sit back
and take it all inside,
For you may be a butterfly simply waiting to arise.

SOARING

Shoot for beauty in your day-
dreams and quietness at night.
Standing on a promise and living for what is right.
Hold your head up high as you
soar through the sky ...
The ones who fail the most in life
are the ones who never try.

IF

If I had the desire for love, it would
be for that of a superior race.
Unimagined royalty.
Sometimes I find such moments of sheer
bliss that I cringe with excitement and
wring my hands until they bleed.
Other times I writhe in pain
and wrestle on the floor.
What is life that one derives to conquer it so?
And what is love but intuition imagined?
What is thought but imagination reinvented?
And touch but lack of vision?
Ordination and innovation are knock-
ing at my door, but me, poor soul
that I am, cannot hear anymore.

SPRING

My thoughts serenade the coming of
spring...my soul's adrift with love.
I cherish sweet refreshing hours
worshiping God above.
A precious scent lingers about, and from
where it comes I know...it comes from the
Lord on high and from His majestic throne.
I prance around to and fro without a
doubt or fret...I dance with twilight as it
falls and am bound with no regrets.
The dogwoods sing, and I, their
friend, smile and sing along.
Such a joyful tune is this and such a joyful song.
The hours pass, but I'm quite
numb to the hands of time.
And so I sit complete in deed with
radiant thoughts in mind.

HE PROVIDES

Tainted and tarnished...she travels through days—
Bent over in worship...her hands upraised.
She calls to her God and cries on her knees.
Begging for crumbs...He provides what she needs

MOSES

When Moses was a baby, Pharaoh's
daughter took him in.
She found him in a stream and
raised him as an Egyptian.
As he grew he had the best that life
could offer him, but as he grew he
also saw injustice in the land.
He fled into the desert after murder-
ing a fellow man, then one day God spoke
to him and said, "I Am that I Am."
"Free My people and let them go, for I have
heard their cry," is what the Lord would
have him say to Pharaoh in due time.
Moses argued that he was slow in speak-
ing and declined, but the Lord gave him
strength and many wondrous signs.
Pharaoh didn't listen, as you know the story well,
it took many miracles, but the Egyptian army fell.
We all have a mission no matter how
small or inadequate we may feel.
There are people who need our
help, so let your spirit yield.

JOSHUA

After Moses died, Joshua took charge.
He led the people of God's
camp on a noble march.
He led them over Jordan and to the
Promised Land…victory was through the
Lord and through His mighty hand.
The story of old Jericho, the trumpets and the fall were simply because of
obedience to the Creator of it all.
The Promised Land exists today
as it did back then,
All He asks is that you give your life over to Him.

THE MASTER PLAN

In the beginning all was dark,
until a light shone through.
A thought was found in the mind of God
and the thought was of loving you.
The galaxies formed, twisted, and
turned, but the best was yet to come
On a planet we would dwell cherished by the Son.
The living creatures were given names
as humans found a home.
All of a sudden the great I Am
no longer felt alone.
He had his mates so pure and true
perfection was at hand,
But then came Satan into the garden as choice was given to man.
Would they follow the Lord of
Hosts and their closest friend?
Or would they fall, temptation bound,
into the tempter's hands?
There came decision and that with
regret for that the great woe of man,
But thank the living and only
One, He had a master plan.

He gave His Son for all who'd believe to join Him once again
In the blessed communion they shared before sin entered in.

DILEMMA

Some people come here...they
trample the ground.
Unbeknownst to them...beneath what is found.
A fountain of pleasure for all who receive...forbidden fruit for those who deceive.
It comes in many forms...it comes in many
ways, but if it does come, best not turn away.
So here's the dilemma, it's still true today...you
can follow the Lord or just walk away.

SOME MOMENTS

Some moments I've witnessed
beauty in its truest form.
These are moments that stand out from
the rest for they are not the "norm."
There are times when everything's
right and you're glad to be alive.
You feel as if you are glow-
ing and flickering inside.
I taste purity in the sky while
absorbing rock and trees.
Oh, how pleasant serenity and the
joy these moments bring.
I collide with the sun while lying here alone, oh,
the splendor of it all...the earth a shapely home.
Majesty comes in bursts and disap-
pears just as fast, but trouble cannot find
me here amongst the leaves and grass.
And so some moments leave a mark
with none other to compare.
I am left only to thank the Lord
for moments quite so fair.

THE ONE

I never want you to lose your zeal.
I never want you to lose your passion.
I never want you to lose your "cool."
I never want you to lose your fashion.
I always want you free.
I always want you fun.
I always want you never chained
but always able to run.
You will always be my shooting star,
you will always be my sun.
You will always be my night and day,
you will always be "The One."

HE MEANS THE WORLD TO ME

He has angelic features with sunlight in his hair.
He has a brilliant smile that whispers not a care.
His eyes are such that radiate love
and his heart is so ablaze ...
With all the wonder of a child he
traipses through each day.
I often question how a man can be so very free.
All I know is that this man
means the world to me.

A BETTER LOVE

Words of life speak to me in dreams I can't recall.
Time stands still in the past...reminded of the fall.
I remember a fleeting moment, sewn up in history.
Counting stars beneath the dawn,
the moon shone down on me.
Sorrowfully I lay with you, know-
ing our time would end,
But in the distant future, a bet-
ter love would round the bend.

SHE WILL NEVER TELL

Her hair is golden brown.
Her skin is dark and burned.
Her eyes are on the ground
As the sky comes tumbling down.
There is a peace she knows far beyond this town
Amongst all the raging waters of earth
she digs in the mud-trod ground.
She holds on to life and gives it all she's worth.
She plays in the dandelions and drinks up the dirt.
She frolics in the blue with
sweat and soiled hands.
She understands the secret to life unlike any man.
Wild is this thing called life, and,
oh, she knows it well,
But to share the secret is some-
thing she will never tell.

WHERE I START

The joy that I've enthroned
The sorrow that I've known
The knowledge I've been shown
And the hope that I've bestowed
Leaves me empty with the thought
of gladness in my heart, and
so I circle timeless words, finishing where I start.

PURE LOVE

In the morning and evening
hours when I'm all alone.
I celebrate the gift of life and
all the love I'm shown.
I think of days yet to come and
ponder days of old,
Contemplating every one as if they are pure gold.
The sky's aglow with pinks and blues
and I'm thankful for today.
I sip a coffee and search for words to
explain—this feeling I have, so free and
true...a gift from God above, and so I witness a rebirth hinged around pure love.

A Brief Encounter with Creativity

Sifting through emotions—segregation thoughts of reality.
Marmalade breezes and fields of wildflowers.
Rolling hills of pleasure as far as the eye can see.
I recline softly on blankets of green while
birds above grace the air in flight.
The rushing of a spring nearby
brings with it peace of mind.
Such wonder, such enchantment.
A world unknown to many...I bask in serenity.
Much pleased with my newfound creation I shall visit here often but regretfully must draw this first visit to a close.
I open my eyes and am thrust back into my office
on 2nd Street to face the hassles of daily living.

AFRAID

I want to do something differ-
ent—I want to be a nun.
I want to walk through air—I
want to feel the sun.
I want to be an astronaut flying into space.
I want to feel the serenity of a
loved one's close embrace.
I want to count the stars while lying on the shore.
I want to do something different—
I want to do something more.
I want to be an eagle soaring through the sky.
I want to do so many things,
before it's time to die.
I want to climb a mountain just to feel the rush.
I want to paint a picture without using a brush.
I want to walk on water but am afraid to try.
So I'll just sit and I'll just dream
and watch my life pass by.

AWAY WITH YOU

The trees are swaying in the wind.
The water is cool and moist.
Gentle words flow from the
heart...nothing felt is forced.
So easily thoughts come to mind,
like thoughts so pure and true.
The only thing I am missing now
is to float away with you.

LIFE

Green is the color God chose for the
seed-bearing trees of earth.
Brown was the color of Adam when
God first gave him birth.
Now the seed of the earth is life and Adam
represents the same...for through his blood
the Savior came who died and rose again.

MENTAL SIGN LANGUAGE

Trapped behind algor bars of self-denial—
confined...the result of emotions suppressed.
Contentions are much whiter still than harbored dissensions, internal displeasure.
Upon the grounds of communication, a developmental state of mind is formed, but unfertile soil becomes a prison of pretense.
Early frost on relationships dawning brings
to life infectious growth, while grief's brother
sits on the doorstep of unspoken words, but
inquisition's heart and mind gives unexpressed
emotions life and thus, life's book poetically
authored, becomes more than just your interpretation of another's mental sign language.

DIVINITY

Days are dim but life with him
is always fun and free.
How divine is this love given unto me.
Placid clouds dance in the sky
as valleys are in view.
How much joy I feel while lying here with you.

WHISPERING PEACE

How can joy array a face when
tears come streaming down?
All the sorrow of the years so readily abounds.
In the mind of one so young sheer
brilliance is displayed,
Thoughtfully the child squeals as joyfully it plays.
The Savior fills her heart with love as
she tiptoes through the stream,
Never questioning the world
around as her soul it sings.
Her mom and dad, they fight again,
but she's the one who pays.
Escaping from reality her timid spirit prays.
He speaks to her quietly, whispering peace,
and so in her hardship she still finds release.

ALL THAT'S DISPLAYED

I speak to the day as the earth to the sky.
The whispers of love are all floating by.
Youth begets laughter as light to the globe.
Spring is alive while beauty is shown.
Within the mind of a spirit aglow
The Father brings sunshine into all that I know.
And so I'm content with the peace that's arrayed
And wonderfully happy with all that's displayed.

A GIFT

He has compassion in his eyes,
he's barely ripe with age.
He has a sordid history, which he
scribbles down on page.
His smile is that which can lighten
hearts and make a woman squirm
Within her seat. He has the skill
to offer her lessons learned.
He is a master in the art of deal-
ing with romance...he can make you long
for him, willing to take a chance.
He has charisma with a charm
that delves inside of love.
He is a child, hardly a man, but
a gift from up above.

ON BENDED KNEE

Reeling with laughter I drifted away within
the beauty of a bright summer's day.
I lay with the sun on an uneven earth and
gave myself time to give myself birth.
My spirit was dressed with a fragrant bouquet
of daffodils and lilies in the place where I lay.
I lowered my head and on bended knee I
felt Him draw near and whisper to me.
He spoke of the beauty the orchard displayed,
He spoke of the flowers and went on to say
that worry was far, no care was abroad, joy-
fully He hummed me a heavenly song.
Our day in the garden was so pure and so kind.
He spoke to my soul and spoke to my mind.
Soon it was twilight and I had to go, but I still
feel His spirit and I want you to know that no
matter how distant dear Jesus may seem, He's
there in the garden waiting for you and for me.

TIME AND TIME AGAIN

I've never felt freer than with a pen in my hand.
I parade around joyously—devouring land.
I wrestle with toils, I wrestle with tasks…but
have found that writing helps me relax.
So I ponder, contemplate, and pray for
thoughts to flow—oh, shimmering day.
Nightly perception and sought-after thrills
keeps me reminded of just what is real.
I've relearned the truth and what it's about,
leaving no room for worry or doubt.
So experience your mind and the spirit within and
you will find happiness time and time and again.

MY WAY

My life was an endless maze...my
eyes were blinded by haze.
My days were filled with pain
until you called my name.
You pulled me out of darkness and
brought me to the light.
You showed me what love really was
and taught me what was right.
True on the path that I ventured
down there were fun and games.
But I wouldn't be alive today if
You hadn't come my way.

WITHIN MY SOUL

The earth and sky do collide on the distant sea.
I feel the water—cool and
moist...as it beckons me.
To its edge, to its shore...no other heart can know
The joy and comfort I feel here and
have found within my soul.

THE ULTIMATE STORY

The idea is born—more and more distant from the world I become...separate.
Fire, a burning desire consumes me.
Exhausting, yet exhilarating energy
flows through onto paper.
Bits and pieces of who I am—etched forever.
Desperate and longing for completeness, I write on.
The life created becomes more and more real
with each word, phrase, soon replacing reality.
Nothing more invades my mind—characters
day and night begging for finished destinies.
Agonizing torment, yet free expression combine to flood every crack, crevice of my being.
Day—night the plot grows in my mind.
A page left unfinished leaves an emptiness of soul.
As the last page is scribbled, only one word is
found to describe this feeling...accomplishment.

THE HEAVENS ABOVE

Gently, noble, shimmering breeze gives
birth to reason and sets my soul free.
In a world of right and wrong...I truly
feel blessed and truly belong.
The sun is aglow and bathes me, it seems, in
the warmest of midday and sings to me.
It sings of a time when there'll be no more pain.
A time in the future when
there'll be no more rain.
And so I bask in the shadows of love...thanking my God for the Heavens above.

THE UNICORN

There once was a girl who lived by the sea...who laughed and who loved and who vividly dreamed of being a horse...a unicorn, in fact ...
She escaped in her mind, never wanting to come back to a world that seemed cruel and dark. She only wanted happiness to fill her young heart.
So she played upon her knees, for
when she frolicked she felt free.
Then something happened.
She found reality.
She learned that her world was all make-believe.
Unicorns weren't real, they didn't exist, and so the life she lived was nothing but a myth.
She grew into a woman and put childhood behind, but she will always be a unicorn inside.

MY LOVE

I was down and you picked me
up...you made me feel like gold.
I am thankful I have you to honor,
to cherish, and to hold.
You make me feel complete in so many ways with
the little things you do or the little things you say.
You are the kindest man that I ever could have
met...you ask me sometimes if I ever have regrets.
Not for a moment, not for a day, I only
hope I can truly repay all the love that's
been shown me...all the love I've known.
Since you've come into my life,
I've done nothing but grow.
And so I want to thank you, but words
don't seem enough, and so the only way
I know is to show you with my love.

By and By

The butterflies land upon my head—
the grass beneath...a delightful bed.
The flowers around make no
sound...such a joyful day is found.
So bright and sunny it calls to me...gently humming, whispering glee.
Grand, indeed, is this simple gift...a
day ordained with a simple kiss.
Weary travelers such as I...find
weary rest in this by and by.

JOB

God wasn't mad with Job…it had been
a cosmic test between Satan and our
Maker to see who was the best.
Job lost his family, his children, and his sheep, but
Job held on strong to the Lord and to his belief.
Job said to God, "If I have done any wrong, then
why do I feel righteous and am able to stand
strong?"
He sought to hear straight from the
mouth of God what he had done.
His friends couldn't help him when
to visit they had come.
Job knew he was innocent and was
guilty of no sin, so the Creator answered
him and restored him in the end.

THE CHOICE

Life is good, meant for enjoyment. I
never intended it to become a burden.
I am broken in your discontent. You are
not satisfied with my gift of life? Why?
What could I have done differently that would
have pleased you more? You bring burdens and
sorrows upon yourself. I have created the whole
earth for your enjoyment. I have given you the
entire universe. Every living creature I created uniquely for your entertainment. The birds
sing for you, and seasons change to prevent
your boredom. No two sunrises are alike…each
hand-painted to please you. The ocean contains mysteries never fathomed by the human
mind…all created so you would never tire in your
adventure on earth. Why are you not pleased?
Why does my creation run from me and despise
me without cause? What wrong have I done that
you would turn from me without reason? All
this I have done for you…because I love you. I
loved the thought of you even before I gave you
life. Joy consumed me as I imagined you walking
through my creation in awe of its many wonders,
exploring all that was made for you. One thought

played in my mind more than any other. It was the thought of the blessed communion we would have with one another, the intimate relationship we would share as a father to his child. Tears of joy flooded my eyes on the day of your birth. I stood watching overhead, proud of my perfect creation. I saw your first steps and watched lovingly as you spoke your first word. I sent my angels to mend your scraped knees, and I kissed your forehead as you lay in bed sick. I provided your every need. You had no fears or worries about the future. I watched you grow. I watched as you played by day and was at your bedside as you slept. I also watched as your heart began to grow cold and the innocence of your youth faded. I wept for you as you continuously gave into temptation. How I desired to tear down the walls that you had built around your heart to everyone and everything...to me. How could something created so perfectly go astray? I watched in agony as you gave yourself up to evil desires and selfish ambition. You craved self-glory and power. You were never at rest, always searching, yet you never came to me. Had you a glimpse into the unseen realm you would have found me standing at your side, eager to comfort you if only you would have asked. You see, when

I created you, I gave you a choice. If I made you love me, than that wouldn't be love. Instead I let you make the decision I won't go against your will and force myself upon you if you don't want me. My heart aches as I think about the way things were supposed to be, the loving relationship we were to share. I look at the earth and remember the excitement that swept over me as I pictured you exploring and loving the world created for you. Yet now I see you wake up in the morning and go through the day as if you were blind. You take each day for granted and every gift I continue to lavish upon you, such as food, shelter, family, and countless other blessings. You spend each day worrying about the next as if you control them. I provided for you your whole life, why start to worry now? How can you think I know nothing about your day-to-day activities and think I don't care? You refuse to ask me for help. If you could see the tears I've shed for you and how I long for a relationship with you and how you're always on my mind, then would you come to me? I'm never too busy for you. In fact, I did show you how much I care. I put myself in a human body and came to earth to tell you what you otherwise couldn't know. Even then, when I personally told you, you still wouldn't believe.

I even gave my life for you. I took upon myself the very sins that you had loved more than me. I paid the price for what you did and you still turn away. What have I ever done besides love you? I will never hurt you or abandon you. I can bring you peace. You were created to have a relationship with me, and you will never find true contentment until you join in that which you were made for. You can't fit a circle where a square should be, which is what you have been trying to do. Only I can fill the space. How long will you continue to search when I have already given you the answer? You have nothing to lose and everything to gain. I will never let you down. I have loved you since the beginning of the world...even before, and I will never stop loving you.
The choice is yours.

VICTORY

Darkness surrounded the cover of night,
what foreign being had entered my sight?
Ghastly it was with two horns and a tail,
conquering my joy until it prevailed.
It laughed, and it sneered, snarled, and shrieked,
"Where is your God this night as you sleep?"
I had no response, I felt at a loss, I had been
battling doubt while carrying my cross.
All of a sudden Jesus appeared, he placed
His hand on me...I had nothing to fear.
He held up the other, and the being
grew weak. The nailprints were clear;
the demon knew he'd been beat.
He recoiled quickly, hissed, and then fled. The
battle was over, he'd been reminded again.
I went off to sleep with Heaven in mind,
serenity and peace filled me inside.
You may face battles and feel you have lost, but
always remember victory is yours at the cross.

MY YOUTHFUL GAME

If I were a child, I would carelessly
drift away to a place where innocence
bathes beneath the light of day.
Strawberry fields and nectar-
ines would always be in bloom.
Night would never enter in, only
the brightness of afternoon.
I would play with dolls, teddys, and
beads, then pour a cup of tea.
Alice in Wonderland would never
have anything on me.
I would surround myself with color, the
kind that never fades, and then invite all of
mankind to join in my youthful game.
We would dance and sing, frolic and
laugh, for all things would be new.
All it takes is a childlike heart
and the rest is up to you.

DREAMING

Salty water echoes through clouds.
Pinpointing darkness the moon looks down.
The water is calm and on the shore
The tide flows in and covers the floor.
Appearing as diamonds the sand looks serene
And so I recline...alive just to dream.

ONCE

Once upon a time, so very long ago,
I played among the dandelions in
fields where they did grow.
I found release, for all was pure,
there was no darkness.
Beneath a pine I wept for love
and found a heart for Him.
I felt the sun shine on my neck as barefoot
I did tread through the meadows, whispering glee while fragrance played out in song.
Time stood still as I did climb onto
the river's edge; there in beauty I collapsed beside the joyful ledge.
My toes they danced beneath the light
of all that youth had wrought.
Not a care was found in me, not a simple thought.
Years have passed, but youth
remains and is as dear to me
As the fields I found in love mingled with ecstasy.

ONLY TIME WILL TELL

She believed in Heaven, while he believed in hell.
She believed in Jesus, while he believed in spells.
She believed in loving God,
while he believed in sin.
She believed in Scripture, while
he believed God is within.
She voiced her beliefs on earth, while he
kept his inside...so on the day of judg-
ment there was no place for him to hide.
All her life she spoke of love, while
he spoke of other lives.
She died and went to Heaven, while
he found the other side.
So which one will you choose this day?
To follow him or her?
Better make your mind up now
which master you will serve.

ADAM AND EVE

When Adam and Eve bit into the apple,
God said, "Don't despair—for from your
line will come a Savior and an Heir.
When He comes, He will rule with justice
and with grace, and although we're separated
for a little while, you again will see My face.
You see what Satan meant for evil, I meant
for good...I know you hearts and minds,
my loves, I know you've misunderstood.
You were born with curious minds and will realize in due time, the apple wasn't an accident but
was part of My perfect plan for children of My
own one day who would love Me and understand.
So because He gave His life for you, being
My only Son...today you can walk with
Me again and live with Me as one."

THE AUTHORED LIFE

What more is an authored life than the exercise of mental imagery—a workout of sorts?
Shakespearean thoughts entwine with
Poe to become the physical manifestation of the mind's eye.
Catapulting sequences of experience combine with self-exploration in birthing a
poem—the "Carrier Pigeons" of expression.
Kingdoms of emotion are built on the
foundation of internal explanation.
How peculiar to me—the life of an
author...suppression must have been
found somewhere along life's way.

INFATUATION

Do you ever think of me?
Am I often on your mind?
Not a day goes by without a sim-
ple thought of you in mine.
A smell, a sight, a sound—
Somewhere,
Somehow,
Sometime,
Brings to life the dream of you and
two lone hearts entwined.

ANOTHER SUMMER

I remember those days ...
They were free—didn't know where
we were going... didn't really care.
It seemed all night your head rested upon my lap.
I wanted to keep going, keep driv-
ing... never to stop.
I wanted to take you that night
and leave the world behind.
I wanted to run.
The fuel gauge marred our plan, and
so we went home to bed instead.
Ah, but I remember those days.

ANOTHER POEM FOR MOM

She is never more beautiful than when she laughs.
She smiles and I smile.
She is dressed in white linen again and hangs
around the stars this cool November eve.
How can I convince her of love that
lasts for more than a day?
How can I convince her of song
when she can't afford to play?
She talks with God over how polite the
weather has been and falters into sleep.
She melts with the ocean sometimes and
gives her heart away, but how can I convince
her of love that lasts for more than a day?

FLIGHT OF SENSES

Can I calculate emotion?
Can I predict forthcoming words?
Has a poet ever done so much?
I explain myself nothing...lost
upon a canopy of delight.
Softness fills me now.
Momentary bliss by touch entertains rea-
son, and so I am gone...carnality misplaced.
The world is now a friend with pleasures to ensue.
And so newness finds her-
self in this "Flight of Senses."
But heaviness sets in—the kiss has
ended and the flesh returns.

THE VISION

The Lord came to me in a vision one
day and sat down by my side.
I felt my soul reveal itself, there
was nothing for me to hide.
He said, "I know your journey's long, my
child, and tough the battle lines, but in the
end you will see for you what I had in mind.
"Though you cannot always see Me, I am
closer than a friend, and if you remain in
My love, I'll be with you till the end.
In the valleys it's hard to see, but
here come the mountaintops ...
Don't worry about climbing too
fast...I've removed all the drops.
Though you may grow weary, never
doubt or fret, for in your life My will is
done, I'm with you, don't forget.
If you ever wonder, am I still looking out? Know
your prayers are heard, My child, you don't have
to scream and shout."
After this He fled my sight and I went
my merry way, but never will I for-
get the chat and all He had to say.

WAITING TO LIVE

Agitated!
Agitated I sit.
I sit and wait.
I sit and wait for what I do not have.
I have not that which I wait for.
Agitated!
How long must I wait?
I must wait long.
Long waiting.
Agitated!
Agitated! Agitated! Agitated!
I could not wait, yet waited still—
Then I died...unfulfilled.

RESISTANCE

Could he for the summer's day resist
all her charms that fell his way?
Or for the sake of Heaven's light
remain a virgin in her sight?
If it were me, and I'm not you, I'd look
way on past her and farther on still.
She's dressed in red, you know what that means.
Here comes the downfall to many of his dreams.
Mighty men have fallen asleep in her arms.
Oh, will he stand strong or fall to her charms?

ONCE AGAIN

There is no more laughter in the world.
It died with Mozart or Beethoven
and seems to be no more.
If it exists, it is stored up for drunk-
ards or evildoers of the world.
When will the righteous get their share?
I pretend to know about many things but still
can't figure out why the fatherless go hun-
gry or why the orphaned do without.
Why is it that the simpleton is more approved
than the hard-learned master, and why do
the proud brag about their high stature?
When will the righteous get their share?
Rise up, oh Lord, and do not be
weak as some know weakness.
Rise up and give us what is right-
fully ours, what is due our name.
For Your name's sake, do not be slow but
come quick to save, for we drown in our sor-
rows and eat the dust of our flesh.
We are but mere men.
Turn Your eyes to us and make us smile
once more, our Helper and our Friend.

Rise up and give us laughter, Lord, please once again.

A POEM FOR LOVE

Sweet spirit, I know you…or want to.
You touched me and I quivered beneath
your caress…a stranger to your world.
Gentle…gently you embraced me
and I floated through you.
You speak and my heart understands…or wants to.
Naturally drawn to freedom…you seduced
me with a childlike purity of heart.
I weep beneath such transparency.
I weep beneath perfect vulnerability.
Surely you've felt this way before, I feel it in my
heart—the heart that breaks beneath your stare.
Your flaw of love is flawless in its own naturality, but your love is far too vast and your heart
is much too wide…although you land now
for a moment—you will always need to fly.

THE COLOR SPECTRUM

Crimson...the color of the rose that lay at his feet.
Black...murky waters abound—his darkness.
Green...the grass that padded his walk
through the warm spring day.
The day why, it is so alive...so full of color!
Blue...the sky above.
White...the purest of all colors—the clouds.
Red...the wooden bench he
rested on along the way.
Brown...his only companion—the dog at his side.
Gray...a bird perched nearby sing-
ing wildly for crumbs.
Colors...blue, green, gray, red.
No matter—the man has been blind since birth.

DESIRE

And so it is the quiet ones who shout the loudest, "Give me my whips, where are my chains of indifference that bind me to the children of tormented rapture?"
Bearing ground, they pause and have a thought.
"What if they come to us…the ravenous beasts of wanting?"
They pause again …
"Let them come."

DAYS IN THE RAIN

The girl downstairs in the pretty skirt
handed me a cigarette and some change.
What I really wanted was to
drink and waste away.
Never having composed a song or exposed myself
to the "God of experience," I was of a tender age
with all the wifely virtues but a needle in my arm.
I always wanted to climb but
never had the right shoes.
Ignoring how the birds empty the sky at noonday,
I held the "God of my idolatry" for an eternity
it seemed before I found out it had an end.
I lay in the hospital and remem-
ber you changing the sheets.
I never got to thank you for the song you
sang or the holding of my head to liquid.
I loved you that day, like all the others.
You've come and gone but never
out of heart or mind.
I hope you took a piece of me
with you when you left.

THERE'S ALWAYS TOMORROW

Why is it that so many people in this world
frown when smiles are just as free?
The ocean smiles and is alive with possibilities.
She tickles my tummy and I kiss her forehead.
She belongs to me now, the lady in white.
She folds herself over onto a blan-
ket of blue and whispers my name.
"Come play with me until the sun falls down.
Share your heart now and I will
never let you leave."
But daylight has fled and I'm wet so I depart.
There's always tomorrow.

RETIREMENT

How now can I write of lovely things?
For my heart is content in that.
Puppy dogs and butterflies...I walk in daisies.
Memory past at last—and I hold con-
tentment if only for a moment.
Three precepts of thought and sphere—
I find I'm all the happier here.
My days are long but filled with sun,
my life much better spent.
I have the music of the fields...I've
found retirement.

CHASING THE DRAGON

I have battled with addiction in life and
found refuge at my mother's breast.
The monster has me again and
I know I've hurt you.
I'm sorry.
Off into the night I go.
Off into the rain.
I can't touch bottom.
How do I beat him, this monkey on my back?
I see a friend and relapse in my mind.
I know I am stronger than that…stronger than the calling storm.
I said good-bye yesterday, but here I am again,
maybe for support or maybe just for supper.
I miss the way I saw the sun and
counted constellations in the sand.
I've become a slave to illness, and I cannot sit still.
They are ever calling for medication
here…medication and a new life—
Maybe I will draw an ace.

MY GARDEN

The garden is ripe with the flavors of
spring, and I delight within this day.
Ferociously I toil and spin while
the marigolds all play.
I pause for a moment to thank the
Lord, for the sunshine and the rain.
Then continue the task at hand
while subconsciously I pray.
I know He gives the bounty, the increase,
and overflow, and so I thank Him for his
love that allows my garden to grow.

NEVER AS BAD

Every now and then, when I'm feeling down ...
I look to the sky above and see blue all around.
The forest has a scent, a laughter you can taste, a
joy that only God can bring suddenly finds a way
Into this cold and darkened heart, there
shines a glorious beam and so I real-
ize nothing is ever as bad as it seems.

THROUGHOUT THE YEARS

Broken cages
Prison bars
Soulful longings
Painful scars.
Blessed communion
Wayfaring hearts
Beautiful Savior
Bound from the start.
Glorious Lover, Glorious Son
Glorious Jesus, Glorious One.
Bring us to laughter, bring us to You
Bring us to Heaven when this life is through.
Fill us with joy, and fill us with peace
Fill us with sunshine we beg of you, please.
Renew us through worship,
renew us through prayer
Renew us through spirit as we give you our cares
Promise us each waking hour
that you will just be near,
For all we need is in Your hands
throughout each coming year.

NOT IN VAIN

If I could grasp the coming of spring or understand why a mockingbird sings, then maybe I'd understand the meaning of life and not be afraid to taste and to try—all that's before me and all that's behind is as pointless to me as the words in this rhyme, but there is a time to let it all go and to choose your own path while your spirit's aglow. So relish these hours spent in the rain realizing nothing done for Him is in vain.

SOMEONE LIKE YOU

I see my children in your eyes
I feel my future floating by.
Milky white your flesh to mine
Don't want to rush it—love takes time.
Sweet caresses your hand in mine
You slowly embrace me and fill my mind.
You fill it with thoughts so pure and true
I'm thankful to have found someone like you.

NORTH CAROLINA

I saw him in the sand and the
sun set upon his back.
He said, "Hello," and my past flew away.
He's never been to Brazil, and he's
never seen eyes quite like mine.
I knew he was free, and I wanted his
hands...they could draw and make me cry.
He told me his name...it was for-
eign and hard to spell.
I knew I could live with him forever and we'd
never own a house...but I want a horse.
He loved dogs and talked of Greek
mythology...he quoted Plato.
He spoke symbols with his eyes and his
touch formed colors in my mind.
He loved my thighs and women so I
let him draw me and mold me.
I never felt beautiful before that day...the
day he kissed my hand and walked away.

AFRICA

My bronze beauty calls to me, her name is Africa.
Carpeting her spirit is a tribal song of love.
The sunshine is her friend and col-
ors light her life.
She has seen her share of heart-
ache, of worry, and of strife.
She seems so far away but her
pain is real and near,
And so I bow my head in prayer that
her troubled land will heal.
The starving cry in vain without a crumb to eat.
Epidemics, famine, and plagues
flood her crowded streets.
But there is a God who knows all her fears.
Someday He'll come and remove all her tears.
She will jump for joy on that day,
sing, and dance around,
For there will be peace at last when
the last trumpet sounds.

NATURE

In the leaves, a home I've found…nestled in pines I drink the sound
of a lake, by its shore…I bathe in pleasure and ask for more—
Of its splendor my earthly delight,
nothing blemished is in sight.
The lake is serene, placid at best,
and so I leave all the rest.
The sun is setting, the fog is low, the bees
are buzzing, and the spiders all sew.
Within the forest is a great mystery.
Take time to notice and you will see
that everyday life is not as it seems. Just look
out your window and you will believe.

GLORIOUS GRACE

There exists a place of glorious light, where
angels are shown what's wrong and what's right.
A mystical place far beyond all our reach, in the
mind of a soul that is hopelessly breached.
Between life and death he opens the door and
escapes from reality as he lies by the shore.
Love is renowned here and peace a
sure thing in the world of his hopes
and the beauty of his being.
He remembers the Scriptures
as his spirit flies free ...
His heart holds a promise as he rests by the sea.
Memories are lost here among ancient things, and
time travel is possible in the magic of dreams.
The heavenly creatures and beings so fair
beckon him closer with a brush of their hair.
His life on this earth has come to an end, he
can see Heaven's gate rounding the bend.
Suddenly he's brought back to the sound of a
voice he heard long ago that gave him a choice.
Would he choose Jesus or a life of pure sin?
As the city draws closer, he knows the decision
was worth all the scoffing and ridicule he faced,
for he has been saved by God's glorious grace.

WHAT IS

What is the earth and what is the moon?
What is the sun in bright afternoon?
What is the ocean and what are the fields?
What is this energy that enlivens and heals?
What is a rainbow and what are the stars?
What is true love but that what you are.
What is a smile and what is a hug?
Nothing but majesty shining down from above.

THE DEPARTURE

When I feel my soul within
break beneath your stare,
I count the days till autumn falls
and caress the weight of air.
I whine and weep that love can
be that of joy and peace.
Capturing the moment, I'm
reminded that I'm free.
Nights I spent beneath the moon
never wanting dawn to come.
Find a place in memories past
beside the truth of love.
But dawn did come and that with
force into the blackest night.
You were born for another, my love,
and to leave you was only right.

YOU WILL BE THERE

When the world is dead and gone, "you will exist."
When mankind is no more, "you will be there."
You will be laughing, you will be living,
you will be dancing, you will be giving.
When lovers make their quiet haste
along the peaceful shores ...
You will be there spreading joy, hopeful evermore.

LONELY BOY

For some reason I never saw you with a smile.
You walked the halls...eyes folded down
in some sort of awkward stupor.
Always dropping books and getting funny
looks, your pants were always too high
and your shoes, never the right size.
You never heard the word hello, and I
believe your favorite color was green,
same as me—but then again ...
They buried you in yellow.

HAPPINESS

I smell the nectar in the air and wish I were a bee.
Free to frolic here or there with-
out a want or need.
I'd buzz around the carefree
day…one flower to the next—
and find great joy upon my lips …
sucking happiness.
Ah, to be a rose in bloom would bring such
ecstasy, into a world where butterflies would
hover round about me, but alas, I fear I'm
made for much a smaller thing, and so I must
be content with simply a song to sing.

UNTIL THE END OF TIME

You make me feel like I can dance,
Fly, or simply run.
You make me feel like I'm your earth,
your moon, and your sun.
The stars collided when we met
The planets all aligned.
And so I know our love will last
until the end of time.

A LITTLE LOVE

The world is full of unhappy people.
Lighten their load...lighten their day.
Send them a card or join their charade.
Pick them a flower of give them a hug...there's
always enough time to spread a little love.

VICTIM OF FATE

The small creature abides alone just outside
castle walls—the moat...his new home.
The princess is in view, but the frog prince
is helpless to reach her...a victim of fate.
Weren't all fairy tales supposed to
end with "Happily Ever After"?
Why then do I remain in this unshapely form?
I speak but am misunderstood by human ears.
What happened?
Perhaps the author grew bored with her
writing and quickened to the finale.
In her haste, I was forgotten, and another
on a white horse claimed my bride.
As she scribbled down careless words, was
she aware they were to become my reality?
Did she know the pen in her hand was the God
of my destiny?
Kingdoms awaited my rule, but she
cashed in on my torment.
My eternity—now left in the hands of children, or the mouths of parents at sunset.
Clothed in green, yet a stranger in nature's plan.
I live, but this is not life.

So shall it be—entertaining the imagination of youth for all time.
Perhaps she has a sequel in mind!

THE DAY I NEVER DREAMT

I remember walking along the beach with you.
I remember the nights I spent with you.
The nights I thought would never end.
I love you still like I loved you then—
My friend, my love.
Why did I wait?
We held paradise but only for a day.
I never dreamt you'd leave my life today.
I never dreamt of saying good-bye.
I never dreamt…that day I never dreamt.

MAYBE TOMORROW

Timid emotions flee with the night ...
The rain comes pouring down,
Pelting droplets of mischief and pain.
I listen to the sound.
My heart it beats and is alive
with worry so ablaze ...
Maybe tomorrow the sun will come
out as I long for better days.

A LOVE LIKE THIS

He takes her by the hand as they
walk in magical bliss.
He gently whispers in her ear
sweet nothings with a kiss.
The air is fresh as they make their
way beside the peaceful stream.
The grass comforts their soiled feet
as they joy in pleasant dreams.
Nectarines fill the earth...cherry
trees are in bloom.
Never was there a love like this
on such a quiet afternoon.

YOUR LOVE

The night cradles me within its womb.
The star-filled sky whispers of you.
The evening is lovely and so
warm with the breeze ...
I'm high in this moment with sheer ecstasy.
Embracing you slowly with a look and a glance
I embrace taunting love with coming romance.
I fill up my soul with the gleam in your eye,
And so I know happiness with emotions inside

MOMMY DEAREST

Her face is bright and sunny.
Her hair is tinted gold.
She has a warm enlightened spirit,
With too much love to hold.
I call her teacher, I call her friend...I
call her many things.
She is a woman of hopes and dreams
but always Mommy Dearest to me.

BLACK

Galaxies collide, but where were you
when we kissed beneath Neptune?
Shot out past the Milky Way and col-
lapsed under the sands of Saturn?
Nowadays it's just black holes, every-
thing is black, black, and bleak.
No new life forms here.
The rocket ship has landed and not
on solid ground, yet I tell you to tell
me when no one is around ...
And it's black.

VICTIM OF FATE II

I'm still here waiting alone in my
moat outside my home.
Where's the steed and the husband-to-be?
Is it possible the author remembered me?
Here comes the princess, she's still plenty in view.
All it will take is a kiss or two.
She's walking this way through
the weeds and the fog.
They must have broken up, for
she is kissing a frog.
You wrote it so fast, I could barely keep up,
but up I came out of the mire and muck.
A burst of sheer magic and a prince I've become.
The princess is mine...you wrote it, it's done.
A kingdom now beckons, awaiting my rule,
because of your words and an erase or two.
Thank you, dear author, for your change of heart.
Thank you, dear author, for my fresh start.
Thank you, dear author, for you
time and your bending.
Thank you, dear author, for my happy ending.

WHAT IS REAL

Light reflects the coming of dawn,
when you will soon be gone.
The radiance of the sun overhead evokes a sorrowful yawn.
Here I am in your arms, careening with your hands,
Never wanting to fall asleep for
the moment is too grand.
We ventured through each waking hour,
never knowing which way to go.
So carelessly we traipsed through
days with only love to show.
Two heavenly children in the grass
romping through the fields... .
Never losing sight of Him by living for what is real.

HAPPY NIGHT

Music plays as lovers dine—
All a part of His design.
The wine is sweet as they recline
On fluffy pillows soft and kind.
The rug is warm, the fires lit.
Oh, happy night ...
Retirement.

VICTIM OF CIRCUMSTANCE

Marigolds and butterflies dancing in the night.
Broken-hearted lovers blindly losing sight.
Tiny arms and legs—beneath a stronger force.
Flailing here and there as nature takes its course.

ON HIGH

Bold and beautiful—this star-filled night.
Breaking dusk falls to light.
Memory gone with the past.
Love it hides behind a mask.
Gentle is the blowing wind
As my voice rings out to Him.
I lay beneath the sound of love,
While Heaven reigns from up above.
Morbid dreams are washed away
As I rise to greet the day.

EVERY DAY

Beauty follows after love as rain-
bows to the clouds,
Fetching wayward broken dreams
the sky comes tumbling down.
On a peaceful, quiet sea the fishermen are found
In the boat the nets are drawn with
a catch to make them proud.
They want adventure...the earth to
calm, to hold their souls at bay,
And so they revel in a life that changes every day.

EXPERIENCE

Sacred ground defines the heart.
Virginity was lost from the start.
The timid beauty reclines sweet on
the place where lovers meet.
Submission entered in so light, and
so reborn they gain new sight.
They were young, just seventeen, the core
of innocence was found in dreams.
She was pure and he untouched...sub-
dued by flesh and anchored by love.

UNTIL

Maybe someday when time has
ceased and love is all that is
Distant memories of man-
kind will be held in bliss.
Maybe someday when the earth is
gone and the soul of light is found
Within a spirit that cherishes God
the heartbeat will echo sound.
Maybe someday when peace at
last is forced into our lives
Then perhaps we'll stop and think
and open up our minds.
Maybe someday this dream will
arise and we will live as one
But until that day arrives we'll fight to see the sun.

THE STORM

Lightning flashes in the night... rain
comes pouring down.
A violent storm is seen abroad in the distant town.
Wearily the earth does shake
beneath the darkened sky.
Chaos reigns supreme in life as
moonlight slowly dies.

LADY ESTELLE

By lakes still waters...admired from afar
Stands Lady Estelle with her parasol.
What sadness is in her eyes?
What pain does she hide?
What could have caused such a lady to cry?
From inside a window...across the way—
A painter marvels and cap-
tures her beauty this day.
Oh, how he loves her, for his paintings do show,
But of his affections she will never know.

BLISS

On a quiet and timid earth an idle
mind considers its worth.
In a still and peaceful field a cow-
ering heart yields its will.
By a glowing, glistening stream a radi-
ant spirit speaks of dreams.
On a day such as this, the soul
of a child basks in bliss.
And so she plays within and with-
out filled with laughter in and about.

NO MORE

You never speak an unkind word
to the world around.
You witness beauty in your mind as
the sky comes tumbling down.
The twilight falls at your feet,
the sun and moon obey.
Every wish that you have is realized at midday.
The sun shines bright, the birds
resound to the autumn leaves.
Do you know what a joy you are
and how much joy you bring?
You hold a world within your soul,
the universe in your eyes.
You take galaxies by the hand and
hold planets in your mind.
I love your eyes, a radiant blue,
you have a brilliant smile.
I would climb the mountain peaks
or walk ten thousand miles
Just to catch a glimpse of you and
embrace your tender soul,
And so, my darling, I will love you
until eternity is no more.

ETERNAL DAY

The sun is rising, I see a new day.
I chase away thoughts of yesterday.
Now in the valley of right and wrong
I hold on to hope and cling to the dawn.
I count the stars as night passes by.
I feel the arrival of wings and can fly.
No more worry, no more fret ...
I gain control of a life that was wrecked.
So if you come looking, I will not be found—
I've journeyed to Venus and am no longer around.
I've voyaged long and I've voyaged hard
With the courage to venture beyond my backyard.
I leave you this letter, I leave you this map,
So come, won't you join me? There's
nothing holding you back.
Don't fear to attempt the impossible you face,
but finish the course and finish the race.
You can look right behind you, I'm not far away.
Come live in the moment of eternal day.

NOT ALWAYS RIGHT

All the sounds of summer are
right here at my feet.
From branches swaying in the wind
to dogs barking down the street.
Winter is over, the snow has fled,
and I swim the day away.
I could count the reasons why summer's much more fun to play.
But, oh, to ask my mother sweet, she
would, in fact, decline, such a logic,
such a truth, in fact, frankly deny.
Winter for her is a joyous sight
and a great joy to her mind.
A cozy cabin with fire and tea
is what ease her inside.
So I've argued but to no avail,
she's already set in her ways.
There is nothing I can do or nothing I can say to make her come to reason and make her see the light.
So I just live with the fact realizing that mothers aren't always right.

UPON MY FACE

The sky is a heavy blue...the
wind is blowing through
Embers of uneven snow while
leaves embrace the cold.
Darkened days...merrily spent...sipping a cup of tea.
The song of dawn rustles through
trees and falls gently upon me.
Wayward youth and wayward
truth all spent in disarray.
I absorb within my heart of hearts
the reason for today.
Greatness never mattered to me, but
change in the life of man—
And so if I can touch one soul
and take by the hand
A lost and dying race, I would have found
my place and in the end found laughter wearing a smile upon my face.

HERE

Everything is dreamlike—I enter another sphere.
I sit and search for meaning—
I circle thought in fear.
I have a right to know...I have the right to near.
I sit and wonder above all
else...what am I doing here.

A MOMENT IN TIME

The golden grains of sunshine that cover
all the earth bring beauty to my mind as I
quietly give birth—to a reason far beyond
the perception of all man...lying down on
the ground my heart absorbs the land.
And so in stillness I contain a thought
within my soul to share and to medi-
tate and to forever hold—
The truth that I've found, while resting here alone
can't explain the majesty of what it is I'm shown.

THE LIGHT OF HIS LOVE

The little brown creatures are the only
friends I know…I find them quite pleas-
ant as my spirit inside grows.
Within all reason I capture free thought and
hang on to dreams with stars that I've caught.
The forest is fresh with the scent of sweet pines.
I cling to the hope that eludes captive mind.
I'm sitting in stillness and oneness with God,
thanking dear Jesus for the light of his love.
The dawn is breaking, I see a new day, and
count my many blessings as I fervently pray.
I thank Him for worship, I thank Him for praise,
I thank Him for the spirit that lives in me today.
And so you will find me content with the world
sitting among nature and abiding with squirrels.

UNTIL MY LIFE HERE IS DONE

The ocean plays in my mind.
The waves are calling me inside.
I gently wrestle with Father Time ...
But find release and escape in rhyme.
The boat's afloat and I look at you ...
Remembering all that we've been through.
Not always easy and not always fun, but I
will love you till my life here is done.

SOMEDAY

She has a thousand looks, she
has a thousand smiles,
She has a thousand memories, she's
walked a thousand miles.
She traipses through a world unkind
without a hand to hold.
But when she looks into my
eyes, I see a heart of gold.
How can she live, how can she love
With so much disarray?
How can she carry on and sing
throughout the day?
I often wonder about her past,
what went wrong and why
I wonder what could have
caused such a lady to cry.
I want to hold her, to touch her
face, and tell her it's okay,
But she pulls away inside and brushes off the pain.
Maybe someday her dreams will
bloom and she will find the one.
Until that day I hope and pray
that she will see the sun.

ONCE IN A LIFETIME

Once in a lifetime, that someone comes along, and when you're in that someone's arms…nothing can go wrong.
Then something happens, that true love seems to fade, but you still have the memories and are better off for them today.

GILDED WINGS

Some days I am a tiger, other days I am a lamb.
I take hold of captive thought as
I take you by the hand.
I whisper through the night and
speak of pleasant things ...
Oh, what freedom beckons me
as I soar on gilded wings.

BLATANTLY DENIED

Wherefore comes this sluggard's voice?
How is it that sadness must shout through tears?
Grasping explanation yet blatantly denied ...
I weep.
A paradox of unconsented emo-
tion leaves me weeping.
Desires flee—chasing after the wind
or perhaps the rain—I care not!
Longing is inevitable and yearning inescap-
able, still harmony like sweet melody calls.
Oh, desperation!
Oh, bitter longing!
Sadness and discontentment—
where is your home?
It has been said, "Upon van-
ity's bosom you are found."
Therefore: Deny the self, be kind, and carry on.

THE DREAM

I saw myself as grown and in a house.
There was a gate and a front porch.
I heard my mother calling from the next
room, but didn't pay any attention—
After all, I was grown.

DEEP INSIDE

How can a dream that has no demise
offer a word of encouraging advice?
Or how can a bird that sings out of tune
question a sky that's forever blue?
How can the sun...burning and hot, com-
pare with the moon and its toilsome lot?
And why does a baby smile in jest while suck-
ing and fondling its warm mother's breast?
I suppose not to know...I suppose not to try
To learn all the answers and to question why, but
my brain keeps on searching and my spirit's alive
with plausible reasons that burn deep inside.

WITH HIM

I remember the days of sand and sun
when every flower bloomed.
I was in love with the idea of life and
was madly in love with you.
Possibility was never far as we
made wishes on the stars.
We filled our nights with daring
chance and filled it with romance.
We quoted poems beneath the moon
so refreshing and so white.
Then again, when the sun arose and
I saw dawn inside your eyes.
We are not together now, but I want to
thank you for the time we spent.
Happy hours and happy days
that I won't soon forget.
I am so much older now and the memories are growing dim... I have a different mindset and am glad to be with him.
So I write this poem for you,
just to say with a smile
That I wish you love in life, for you
made my life worthwhile.

CAPTIVE NIGHT

The meadows dance beneath the
sun and we enjoy the fun
Of bathing pleasantly in the fields
before the day is done.
We bask beneath the warmth of
love and dine in ecstasy,
Living for the joy of life and all we aim to be.
Hours pass and I'm alive lying here with you.
The sky above is airy and vast,
an ever-present blue.
We contemplate the light of day,
for it will soon be gone
And so we chant and medi-
tate an ever-joyous song
To these moments in our lives
that seem so very right
Always living for the now by elud-
ing captive night.

ONLY YOU

You walked with the water under your feet, you walked with the Father through rugged streets. You walked through the desert, you walked through the plains, you walked through the fields while proclaiming His name.
No one before you and no one since has preached the word like you and caused repentance ...
In the hearts of the dead and blind men—there was never one like you and will never be again.

ON MY KNEES

Sometimes when the darkness
falls so hard upon my heart
You pull me gently to yourself and offer
a fresh start. Sometimes when I'm lost
and alone upon an endless sea
You gently whisper things that are
true and remind me to believe
That there is a light and there is a
hope that comes from up above.
You bathe me in a sweet caress
and remind me of the one
who came to earth so long ago—
with him the Father was pleased,
and so I repent of all my sins as
I fall down on my knees.

WHERE WE BELONG

So sickening sweet is the fruit of this vine,
but do not eat it or you surely will die.
Such magical bliss we did know before but
now we must leave this beautiful shore.
The garden was lush...the water was pure,
but we were forced out because of allure.
Our spirits died instantly...our bodies in time—
our hearts were darkened and so were our minds.
Envy arose, murder, and greed, but He
never forsook us, He planted a seed.
Within my womb the Savior grew strong and
because of His death we're back where we belong.

ALIVE

The heaviness of life sets in, and
I cry for a dying race.
I realize my own misfortune and
realize my own place.
In a world of right and wrong,
how do people live?
With so much hurting and so much
pain, how can people give?
So demanding is this life with
all the worry and woe.
How can people find the truth and
have wisdom enough to know?
The difference between love and
hate is really a fine line,
And so the only truth I've found
is the truth I hold inside.
The truth about love and light
I hold within my soul.
And so it's easy to survive, hold
on and don't let go.
The dreams you have within your
mind are a gift of the purest kind.
So instead of cursing life, be thankful you are alive.

FOREVER

A gentle moment is spent in peace
while the hours click on by.
The nighttime is a friend of mine
as the stars flicker in the sky.
The moon is bright, the breeze is
soft, and the earth is all at rest.
I savor dawn and daytime too,
but twilight is the best.
I am at one with the world around
as I hold joy within my soul.
The moonlit sky twinkles with love,
the lightning shines like gold.
The storm has passed and the dusk
it rests upon a velvet globe.
These precious moments spent
with God I will forever hold.
Within my soul there is a light
and that to absorb the dark.
And so I know this time will
last forever in my heart.

IF ONLY FOR NOW

What good is a day without the sun?
What good is a life without the one?
What good are flowers if not for a gaze?
And what good are meadows if not to graze?
I hold all these thoughts joyfully inside and
contain a free spirit within my mind.
I search for truth within the lies but am
left uncertain with the answers I find.
So I will contemplate, for this is my lot.
I will keep on searching no matter the cost.
The world will keep on turning regardless of
how, and so I sit satisfied if only for now.

HOW

How can I remember joy when sorrow's all I know?
How can I believe in you when
you've never let me grow?
How can I, in weary pain, tell you how I feel,
When the heart you say you love
is the heart you aim to kill?
How can I, without a smile, laugh jovially,
Pretending all the hurt is gone
that lives inside of me?
How can I without a voice, joyfully hum a tune?
The question is how can I ever
be in love with you?

GOD

I lived inside a poem, I lived inside a book.
The God of my reasoning decided to take a look.
He saw the good, He saw the bad, He
saw the ugly, He saw the sad.
He reached down His hand and pulled
me from above…He taught me many
things but mainly about love.
He said, "This is earth you are here to
share…wherever you look you will find Me there."
He picked me a flower as the
wind blew through my hair.
I looked around…God was everywhere.

WAITING FOR THE DAY

The trees need a home, for the
earth is not their own.
No, it belongs to man, but how
much more can we stand
To take from the globe? No other heart can know
The pain that she feels as she cries unseen tears
And longs for the day we will all fly away.

I'll Be Free

All reason eludes me as I wrestle inside.
I wrestle with pills and wrestle with my mind.
Illness has come to be a dear friend of mine.
I wish I didn't know her but pray that in time
I will see things plainly and be normal indeed,
But until then I will take what I need—to
have simple logic and erase all the dreams.
Living with the hope that someday I'll be free.

WHEN DREAMS DIE

The stargazer grasped.
The stars died.
Fondling failure, the stargazer
cried, and grounded a dream.
Spitting up stars he faltered.
Too many years and too many
tears...the faltering fool!
He gave it life and he gave it breath, then
he faltered and he gave it death.
The stars weren't dead...not as
dead as they seemed.
But faltering steps left faltering dreams.
How close to his dream?
The man never knew...had he
dreamt one more day ...
It would have come true.

SATISFACTION

I examined his energy, studying every gesture, every movement of his character.
This man had something unique to
say, his eyes and spirit said so.
I listened...listened and learned.
I knew he wanted me...wanted me to say
something, but I myself remained silent.
He was serene and uninhibited in
the most natural of ways.
Never crossing his legs, he held my attention and my thoughts, but I wanted more.
I wanted his shoulders...I wanted him.
Not to be this night.
This night was instead dedicated to
the stars...dedicated to the moon, and
so I watched and was satisfied.

COMING OF AGE

Speak to me in truth, being true to what you show.
It seems I see quite differently then
what it seems you know.
Who am I to disagree with what
your heart and mind may see?
Am I not to love you still and
thoughts instilled in thee?
Division and judgmental thoughts,
self-righteousness hath wrought,
But, oh, how beautiful—transparency
and contentment with one's lot.
And so love each life and the difference that
it brings...for time is too fleeting and life is
too short to worry about lesser things.

TOURIST'S PARADISE

Beating circles of drum dance melodies.
They have gathered for the feast.
A lagoon of island dwellers, aroused
by torches of burning incense.
Immense heat, overflow-
ing from the pots of plenty.
Children embrace ancestral manhood.
The beating drums resound with increased
laughter and chanting to unknown gods.
Witnessing this pagan ritual from a dis-
tance—the travelers must have taken a
wrong turn somewhere along the way.

MAYBE

I laughed this morning and forgot to cry last night.
Maybe things are getting better.
The horses that stampeded my mind have all fallen asleep.
They trampled my thoughts but left harmonious tracks.
Maybe things are getting better.
I feel out of touch like the stars at noonday but pour some tea and pray.
Maybe things are getting better.
I'm left here alone but that doesn't bother me...only the fact that he forgot to kiss me good-bye.
Maybe things are getting better.

HEALING

The greenness of trees and the calming of leaves
Brings me to laughter as I fall to my knees.
The blue of the sky, the white of the clouds,
The gold of the sun bathes me in now.
My thoughts are all still, my heart is at rest,
I lay by the stream and truly feel blessed
To be here alone amongst what is real
And so in this moment I take time to heal.

FALLEN

I've tasted Eden in the trees that bid my coming.
I felt beauty one day and held her in sight.
She slipped through my fingers because of wrong
and right, but I owned her and she loved me.
What marvelous bliss.
I was free in her arms and I will
see her again someday.
Someday...I will hear her call.
Someday...when I have been freed from the fall.

HERE AND ABOUT

The uneasy burden of days gone by brings
me to reason as I rest in the sky.
I find simple muse and play with my tongue while
lying and pondering the warmth of the sun.
I bask in its greatness, calming and hot,
but realize my labor and painstaking lot
Is just to know you inside and out and
so I sit satisfied here and about.

DISARRAY

Pious thoughts...captive minds...hours spent a day. Oh, what masks we do corrupt and wear in disarray.

INSPIRATION

I have found misplaced pres-
ence in the form of frailty.
I have found inadequate thought
while capturing reality.
Every bend and twist of knee brings me to the
light.
And so, inspired, I must walk
through colors, oh, so bright.

THE VERDICT

Comprehension falls apart within
reason is the heart.
Life and death it plays a game
with a mind just too insane.
Little footprints on the floor...hard
concrete—behind closed doors.
The child is young and locked away,
put up quick by what they say.
Medication is her friend and so
she longs for bitter end.

IN LOVE

The dolphins swim, the horses
run, and I stampede the sun.
With glorious hours bright
ahead...I believe in fun.
Never a worry, never a care, never an alarming threat of disaster or demise.
I am found content.
And so I sing a song quite new
to my God above—
For I have found what joy life
brings as I am found in love.

WHERE YOU ARE

Label me a failure...label me a loon...label me a victim of bright afternoon.
Label me a wretch...label me a bore...label me a mistress of Heaven's open door
But I will run and I will jump beyond the passing stars and when the earth collides with sun you'll find me where you are.

ALL I KNOW

I manage to believe that all things
thrive in a world of only God.
I lift my hands in tribute for the chorus of
a song that dances plainly for all to see.
The song is Calvary, it tells about creation and the one who died for me.
It tells about a Savior, it tells about
a man who trod the earth a burning fire...forgiveness was His plan.
He lived so long ago, was his life really in vain?
All I know is since His death the
world has never been the same.

I'M SOLD

I love the way you look at me,
your eyes a burning fire.
I love you for all the things you say,
you are my heart's desire.
You make me smile, you make me
laugh, you push away the blues.
I feel like I've found the secret to
life and that is loving you.
You are quite handsome and exquisitely
built with a mind to shame the sun.
You make me feel as if I'm reborn
and make me come undone.
You have this soul, have this charm,
you have a heart of gold.
Let me tell you if you don't know by
now, when it comes to you I'm sold.

INSOMNIA

I tried to sleep inside my dreams but found
that life wasn't all that it seemed.
I tried to rest but found no release...life
wasn't all that it had promised me.
I walked through life half in a daze. I tossed
and I turned but remained awake.
After the torment had grown so loud that
the beating of a drum could not resound...I
sought reclusive quarters inside the crowd
and in the end I finally lay down.

ONLY FRIENDS

Both were afraid to speak so time just passed them by and oceans rushed to the shore instead of to the sky.
Both were afraid to speak...some say they were shy—and so the story ends quite sad and rather with a sigh.

AT HOME IN BED

Some people rise early in life, not
wanting to miss their day.
Other people don't really care,
so lay up in bed and pray.
Many people's lot in life is just to sew some seeds.
That, I think, is the purest kind
and seems like success to me.
So I will sit and I will shine if only in
my head...and when they come look-
ing for me, I will be home in bed.

I LOVED YOU

I loved you every minute, every second of the day.
You always had a joke to tell and
only the sweetest things to say.
I loved you every minute, no mat-
ter where you were.
I loved you every minute...even
when you were loving her.

FACES WITHOUT NAMES

They sit in the pews week after week,
never speaking, never smiling, but you
miss them when they are gone.
You know, the ones silent and somber.
Never mingling, never shaking hands...they
are faces without names...but somehow
you miss them when they are gone.

RHYME

It tasted like pain the way your
tongue caressed mine.
It tasted like rain walking through the sunshine.
I pretended to be a poet, I pretended to be smart.
I wrote all the lines and thought I did my part.
But discourse was found in the sureness of time,
and I was a fool left without a single rhyme.

THE CLOVER

She's a rosebud in the forest.
She's a star passing the moon.
She's a flower you can't help but pick—
She's a clover in full bloom.
She's tomorrow when yesterday's gone.
She's a song with a million tunes.
She's a leaf falling into a pond—
She's a clover in full bloom.
She's a sparrow nursing young.
She's a loved one gone too soon.
She's the apple of her daughter's heart ...
Yes, Mom, the clover is you.

MY FRIEND

I felt the cry of one so dear... whisper softly in my ear.
He told me of hardships... he told me of grief... he told me of lovers who had fallen asleep.
Is it better to laugh or is it better to cry?
Is it better to live or is it better to die?
I think I shall live and I think I shall love.
I think I shall dance with help from above.
So feed me your grief and feed me your woe, but remember, my friend, what you feed me will grow.

LOVE'S LONG PAST

You were boring, but handsome.
You were crazy, but cool.
You were anything but quiet.
You were above all the rules.
I loved each of you in my own special way.
I wouldn't be who I am if I
didn't love you still today.

POETS

Poets mark their past in rhyme,
all ignorant of length,
And can't contain their passion-filled pride so
open up and speak.
Their day is done while wonder-
ing why their ship began to sink.
So given now I hold the notion of
thought and give to think.
Poets mark their past in rhyme...their
future for to hold.
So spitting prose they traipse along
while fondling fields of gold.

THE WORLD DIED

The ocean smiled at me today and the sand
was warm and friendly beneath my feet.
I watched you laughing from a distance…our
eyes met and, "The world died."
You glanced my direction once, maybe
twice before quietly speaking.
"My name is Jack."
You extended your hand.
I couldn't respond, so I smiled
and nodded sheepishly.
You stared at my heart—or was it my soul—
before returning your gaze to my eyes.
You held my stare but had to go,
the water was calling.
You grabbed your board and were off, but our eyes
did meet and for a split second, "The world died."

NOBLE BIRTH

How contemptible a mod-
est world...madness of the hands.
Quickening spirits of like minds,
forever never to plan.
Two lost children amongst the leaves...toss-
ing all cares aside, and in this moment
to truly live and find you are alive.
Later days and later haze marks a
path unknown, but to taste the joy of
life finds noble birth a home!

HOLDING ON TO YOU

The raindrops trickle down my
spine as I absorb the sky.
The ever-present crashing waves
caress me in their tide.
I once held freedom, I once held
peace, I once held harmony.
In the ocean vast and wide I held the soul in me.
I flew away with the dawn one morning long ago.
I remember the joy that I felt… I
couldn't help but grow.
Those were the hours when I knew
that love was really true.
Those were the hours spent in
the rain holding on to you.

THE WINDOW

Oh, to be of noble birth, what sweet ecstasy.
Perpetual bliss—harmony
sings...dramatic melody.
Pick me a flower, sing me a hymn, and tell me
which way to go, because all I can see is darkness now when I look out my window.

LAST

Vanity flies away with dusk.
Air is that of light.
Whispers of forgotten loves
Echo in the night.
Plainly seen in the mind of God
Is a still but silent voice.
Reasoning is a brilliant dis-
play but often a violent choice.
Laughter begets dawn and I, too, my
past always in line at the first
but finishing with the last.

CAREFREE LAND

The sunshine bathes me in its hand
The grass beneath...my only friend.
I sing for joy and use this pen
While love and laughter round the bend.
Rocky streams comfort me as I
whisper taunting glee.
The day is so bright, the hours so grand, and so
I play in this carefree land.

AS YOU

I dance in the rain while the lilies grow robust.
I conquer countless meadows while
the horses trample dust.
In the towns and all around...the
streets begins to crack.
Upon my knees I reason with you
and lie down on my back.
Submission is my lot in life, and so I
rest my head...upon a pillow soft and
white as you climb into the bed.

IF I FAIL

Words can't explain the color of rain or the
anguish of heart when someone is in pain.
It can't describe humanity's brain, they all
run together and sound awfully the same.
I have a constant longing within my
soul that's bound to invent a new language that no other mouth has found.
I need a new verse. I need a new rhyme to
release all the beauty that rests in my mind.
I need a new spirit, a soul that is true, to portray
the word "sky" and a word something like "blue."
I guess I'll keep striving, perhaps all in vain,
but if I fail miserably, I'll try it again.

ETERNITY

I've thought about God and draw a circle.
I come to an end ...
Eternity.

YOU

In the morning I think of you and when the day's ablaze—with love and laughter, I ponder truth and seemingly am dazed...with a spirit so humble and pure—no other soul will do. So you ask me what love is and
I will answer, "You."

SOME SAY

Some say I am blind...others say I can see.
Some say I am chained...others say I am free.
Some say I am wrong...others say I am right.
Some say I'm a coward, and others say I can fight.
It doesn't matter what they say,
for I'm secure in me.
It's never good to judge anyone, so don't label me.

THE NOVELIST

Hating poems ...
Despising the beatnik look.
I want to write a real book.
Nothing to say so I dine ...
Dine and wait for that first line.

YOU

Writing about you makes me feel closer.
Closer to what?
Closer to reading about you.

WRITING FOR THE MIND

Harmonious daydreams and sweet caresses are good for the soul.
But nothing eases a weary body like having your cup overflow.
Mountainous plains and calm river valleys soothe the spirit in time ...
But nothing conquers a poet's heart like writing for the mind.

I AM TOLD

I have to say something different.
I have to say something new.
I have to speak what no one else can
and do what no one else can do.
I have a fire burning inside to
write the impossible poem.
I have to form a puzzle with words so
you will treasure them like gold.
What is verse, and what is rhyme
if not to help you grow?
And so I will do my best to relay
the messages that I am told.

RELEASE

The ocean dances in her head...the
sun shines in her eyes.
She marvels at the earth He made and
has peaceful thoughts in mind.
She pauses for a moment to
send a thankful prayer
To her one and only love, the Creator, oh so fair.
He is the center of her world and
the master of her dreams.
She lives a life of purity and
bathes in pleasant streams.
Sometimes when she's all alone
she feels His spirit speak
To her soul. He whispers truth
and makes her heart believe
In a love so far and vast the universe can't describe
all the wonder of the world that
He holds deep inside.
She cradles birth within her womb,
the beloved of a King,
And so she lives and so she breathes
and basks in eternity.
She doesn't pretend to be above
all that He gives her free.

She realizes in her heart of hearts
it is Him who makes her be.
And so she thanks him every day
for the sunshine and the rain,
Always remembering the day he came
and released her from the pain.

MISERY

Chatter doesn't matter.
Laughter is a farce.
Falling down on broken wings,
piercing at her heart.
Bleeding dawn…memory
lapse…forgotten jubilees.
Sings a wayward concubine of all her miseries.

WHITER THAN SNOW

How do you keep a fool without rhyme walk-
ing in meter and keep them in line?
Or how do you play a game without rules,
escaping mere vanity in all that you do?
How is a mind in a world with just God
placed in the realm of all that is wrong?
And why is the earth bound with regrets
found in the heart of one who repents?
I don't know the answers but find all I need
within the words of a gospel that's free.
And so I am happy with what I do know for
that which I know washes whiter than snow.

HEAVENLY SON

Brilliant night, belittling dawn,
Wayfaring soldiers sing a new song.
The battle is over, the victory's been won
All for the glory of the Heavenly Son.

MAKE-BELIEVE

If I lived in a make-believe world with rainbows all around, I'd dance gaily in their view...cherishing the world I'd found.
If I could for just one day sing a heavenly tune, I'd sing a song for the love of God and send up a prayer for you.
But as it is and as we know, good thoughts are known to pass, and so I relish this ray of light as darkness falls quiet fast.

PERHAPS

Beauty is bound by its master...and I for my love of thee.
Perhaps a makeshift orphan could capture such liberty.

THOUGHT OF DAY

Someone dies and someone lives,
as each new day begins again.
All these thoughts fill my mind
as my soul wells up inside.
The beauty of autumn is never far, embracing dear winter with the bravest of hearts.
Bone-chilling memories and pleasant new dreams are born in the handshake that you seem to bring, but with it comes pain, remorse, and regret, and so counting scars, I would rather forget that dreams often die and memories do fade and so in this moment I escape thought of day.

CAIN AND ABEL

Now Cain and Abel were brothers but
were as different as the moon and sun.
Abel was righteous in the sight of his God
while Cain was the rebellious one.
Abel offered right sacrifices before the living
God, but Cain was known for holding back
and so was corrected when he was wrong.
This aroused jealousy in the heart
of Cain, and so he killed his brother
instead of practicing the same.
He was forced out of the only home he'd
known. Called a restless wanderer by
most, he would be forced to roam.

BIRTH

Evening comes with surprise…mourn-
ing with the moon.
Nights are spent in happy
hours…lying here with you.
The stars they cry but give their
light to the world around.
So complex is this life that readily abounds.
The planets reign from Heaven
above, as do clouds and sky.
Pleasant longings bring release with a quiet sigh.
The birth is real while life is
true…the giver often groans.
Pain is constant in this hour, then the baby moans.

THIRST

The earth is crying for rain
And I am crying in pain.
Emotionally distraught and temporarily insane.
Reaching for a limb, I call out to Him.
Save me from myself...for I am suffering within.
My mind is a mess,
My heart must confess—the sins of my youth
Are thoughts I repress.
My spirit is torn, my face is forlorn—I hear
someone knocking but can't open the door.
The tears they fall down to a thirsty old ground
And so in my sorrow at least satisfaction is found.

e|LIVE

listen|imagine|view|experience

AUDIO BOOK DOWNLOAD INCLUDED WITH THIS BOOK!

In your hands you hold a complete digital entertainment package. Besides purchasing the paper version of this book, this book includes a free download of the audio version of this book. Simply use the code listed below when visiting our website. Once downloaded to your computer, you can listen to the book through your computer's speakers, burn it to an audio CD or save the file to your portable music device (such as Apple's popular iPod) and listen on the go!

How to get your free audio book digital download:

1. Visit www.tatepublishing.com and click on the eLIVE logo on the home page.
2. Enter the following coupon code:
   dbb6-6f11-5003-74a7-d9c8-06ec-7979-c27d
3. Download the audio book from your eLIVE digital locker and begin enjoying your new digital entertainment package today!